ENDORS

ENDORSEMENTS FROM BEST SELLING AUTHORS
AND PROFESSIONALS

Foreword: *Journey into the Looking Glass* by Dr. Mary Welsh

Debra Hayes - *RISE: What to Do When Hell Won't Back Off and 40 Days to Rise: A Devotional to Build A Life Overcoming Disappointment, Heartache and Tragedy*

"It is my pleasure to acknowledge the grief work that Dr. Mary has undergone to address the loss of her daughter, Susie. She uses her positivity, passion, and purpose in life to aid others on a similar grief journey and to brighten and inspire the lives of children and young adults through her nonprofit, Susie Q's Kids.

The essence of her book is simply stated: remember, reflect, recreate, and relate. Remember—share memories and relive them as they are so precious. Reflect—how did your loved one embrace life, how did they impact you and others? Recreate—take their love of life, their passion, and purpose in life, and incorporate it in your own, thus creating your own 'new normal.' Finally, she shows you how to Relate it to your new life without your loved one. How can their legacy live on in the way you live, how can it help you and others, and how can it reflect a positive, purposeful, and passion filled existence?

Let Dr. Mary walk you through these stages and help you celebrate your loved one and embrace your new normal."

Dr. Jeffrey Fisher, M.D.

"Journey into the Looking Glass is a helpful guide full of essential information for those who find themselves facing the loss of a loved one. Dr. Mary Welsh takes the reader through all the decisions, emotions, and situations that the bereaved find themselves having to deal with. This thorough book will not only help you manage the challenges of loss, but help you make peace with it too."

Lisa K. Boehm, author of *Journey to HEALING: A Mother's Guide to Navigating Child Loss* and mother of Katie who died in a car accident at the age of 17
The ABC's of Grief Support: how to help a loved one after loss

"Mary Welsh is very fresh in her grief, having lost her daughter from this earth less than two years upon writing *Journey into the Looking Glass*. However, it is very evident that she has done a lot of grief work in that short amount of time (more than most, I would say). She has gleaned much from a good counselor, marched forward by connecting early to a strong support group with Bereaved Parents USA, and done a *lot* of studying, to be able to put so much information in this book. The array of content is broad, but the chapters are short, which is needed for anyone in the beginning months of grief fog. No matter the loss, there are sure to be some take-away nuggets for the reader in *Journey into the Looking Glass*."

Laura Diehl – Becca's mom
Co-founder and Executive Director of Grieving Parents Sharing Hope (www.gpshope.org)
Host of Grieving Parents Sharing Hope Podcast
Award-winning author of several books, including *When Tragedy Strikes*

"Children are not supposed to die before their parents; unfortunately, thousands of parents are faced with this reality every year. Thanks to courageous moms like, Dr. Mary Welsh, bereaved parents can feel understood and begin the healing process. Grieving is hard work, but through Mary's stories and her suggested action plans, readers can begin to move forward in their grief. The short chapters make this book easy to read and the relevant topics extend the relevancy to anyone who has lost a loved one, not only parents who have lost children. Most importantly, this book allows grievers to see that they are not alone on their journey to self-discovery after loss."

Melanie Delorme, author of *After the Flowers Die: A Handbook of Heartache, Hope and Healing After Losing a Child.* visit MelanieDelorme.com

"Dr. Mary took the tragic pain of losing her daughter and redeemed it into a powerful story of hope for other parents caught in the same experience. She offers a process of remembering, reflecting, recreating, and relating the memory and impact of loved ones. She shows how it's possible to find positivity, passion, and purpose in owning and celebrating a new normal."

Kary Oberbrunner, author of *Your Secret Name and Elixir Project*

"Dr. Mary Welsh captures the essence of the experience of losing a loved one and offers helpful support and encouragement for anyone who needs empowerment to overcome loss. She teaches us how to memorialize a loved one while achieving the power to move beyond the sadness of the loss to embracing the power of a new normal experience without the loved one's presence. I have learned many of the lessons presented in my own journeys of grief and I would highly recommend *Journey into the Looking Glass: Finding Hope After the Loss of Loved Ones* as a companion guide to accompany them along their path to healing."

Marvin Wilmes, owner of Key Publications, The Guild editor, and author of *Beyond the Horizon: Crisis of Faith* and *Chronicles: Journey toward Hope, Overcoming Loss through Faith, Perseverance, and Surrender*

"My relationship as a mystic began with Susie prior to her death. She was always inquisitive of the afterlife and what the future held for her. Her near-death experiences in life allowed us to communicate freely about the afterlife which gave her comfort that when her turn arose, she would be ready. One of her main concerns was whether she would be able to communicate with family and friends, she was comforted that her beautiful spirit would travel both worlds in different manners bringing forth comfort to those she loved. Her positive personality and charm won my heart and enabled us to communicate freely before and after her death. Her spirit is at peace and very active, she is present and sends her signs to let us know we are not alone. Thank you, Susie, for sharing your life with me!"

Wesley Baughman,
Mystic Keeper ™ Clandestine Gardens ®

ENDORSEMENTS FROM BEREAVED SUPPORT GROUP LEADERS AND PARENTS

"I am part of the leadership of a support group for Bereaved Parents. One of the never-ending feelings that haunt Bereaved Parents is the concept of would of, could of, should of. If only I would have done something different, my child would have lived. Parents continually berate themselves with this negative self-talk.

Dr. Mary provides a progressive and positive approach to changing this negative self-talk by replacing the 'What If' statement with 'But I Did' statements. The changing of this internal self-talk is a key enabler in moving forward in the grief journey. Dr. Mary, thank you for providing this inspirational tool."

Kerry Thomas Taylor, in honor of my son,
Erik Thomas Taylor
Chapter Leader, Treasurer of Bereaved Parents of USA,
Macomb County Chapter

"Life goes on without our loved ones; Dr. Mary provides insights to make the journey more self-reflective and to allow for healing to occur. She bared her soul to help others understand they are not alone in their despair and that they will learn and adapt honoring their child's memories."

Christine and Dave DeClerck, in honor of
our son Kevin DeClerck
Co-Leader of Bereaved Parents of USA,
Macomb County Chapter

"Dr. Mary takes you along on her journey, sharing what she learned since the death of her youngest child. Easy to read, inspirational, and the chapters are short enough to hold your interest when you can't seem to concentrate. This book gives advice on how to handle the rough days while helping the bereaved put purpose back into their lives. Every facet of the mourning process is covered with helpful advice and areas to reflect on your own emotions. Hard to put down. Big thumbs up!"

Diane DeClerck, in honor of my son,
Joseph Droste and nephew, Kevin DeClerck
Librarian, Facebook Admin. of Bereaved Parents of USA,
Macomb County Chapter

"Only a person who has experienced the death of a child can understand the pain that grips one's physical and emotional being. Dr. Mary Welsh invites readers to travel with her on this journey of a bereaved parent as she provides hope and guidance for those facing this long and difficult road."

Pamela Leidlein, in honor of my daughter,
Michelle Marie Packard, PhD.
Co-Leader/Newsletter Admin. of Bereaved Parents of
USA, Macomb County Chapter

"The loss of a child is the worst thing that can happen to a parent. Dr. Mary guides you through the different stages of grief and assists one with coping strategies. Life will never be the same without your child, but you learn to develop a 'new normal' way of living."

Paul Serduik and Dr. Halyna Meronek-Serduik,
parents of Andrew John Serduik, JD
Initial Contact, New members of Bereaved Parents of
USA, Macomb County Chapter

"I am the leader of the St. Clair Shores, Michigan Compassionate Friends grief group and found this book to be very intuitive, easy to read, and understanding of the concepts and feelings that each of us as grieving parents in our group wrestle with on a daily basis. Dr. Mary takes us on her journey and lets us relate how we travel a road none of us wanted to roam.

Dr. Mary shares her approach, offers some expertise, and then how she, her family, and friends passed through the different stages of grief. It is her hope that the readers find a commonality, look at the key takeaways, and use the thought questions to document and navigate their own reactions on the way to creating their 'new normal' honoring the past and present. Thanks, Dr. Mary for being so compassionate."

Kathy Joerin, in memory of my son, Mark Ciresi
Leader of Compassionate Friends,
St. Clair Shores, MI Chapter

ENDORSEMENTS FROM PARENTS OF BEREAVED CHILDREN

"None of us as parents asked to join this group, to learn how to live without our children, to find our 'new normal' or to watch other family members and friends hurt. Dr. Mary takes us on her journey with respect for our losses and our loved ones. Her work is easy to digest, small bite-size segments when comprehension is hard, and life is harder. I related to her words describing how to remember our loved ones, my son, as he lived not by any illness, pain, or other circumstance. Thank you, Dr. Mary for sharing your journey and compassion for others."

Dr. Alice Urecht, in honor of my son,
Specialist Keith William Beaupre

"Dr. Mary shared her darkest moments, emotional turmoil, and hopes for making something out of the incomprehensible. She addressed the physical and emotional stress the loss of a child involves. Dr. Mary, thank you, as it was insightful."

Jennifer Millsap, in honor of my daughter, April Millsap

"Life is full of special moments, some full of happiness and others shadowed with sorrow. The loss of a miscarriage or a stillborn birth can be so misunderstood by others, but so real and traumatic to those involved. Dr. Mary, thank you for recognizing all of God's angels in your book and the need to honor them and grieve their loss."

Janelle Benson and Ronny Wilson, in honor of our beloved angel, Tristan Wilson

"Although I have not read the complete book by Dr. Mary, the excerpts that I have read are written to help others cope with the loss of a loved one as well as serve as a loving tribute to her daughter, Susie. As a fellow member of The Bereaved Parents of Macomb, I have seen Dr. Mary make numerous valuable contributions to the group by warmly welcoming new members and encouraging grieving parents in their journey. This book is an extension of Dr. Mary's mission to help others."

Ruth Curtice, in honor of my son, Mark Curtice

"*Journey into the Looking Glass* is a personal reflection of the heart-wrenching journey parents of a lost child have to travel for the rest of their lives. Dr. Mary provides self-help options to understand the stages of grief."

Deanna and Andy Phillips, in honor of our children,
Ellie Marie and Matthew James

"I love how Dr. Mary hits on so many aspects of grief, losing a loved one, and how she deals with the loss of her beloved daughter, Susie. Our precious children should not be defined as how they died, but by the way they lived and what they contributed to life and what they meant to others. If their death and last day was from cancer, a tragic accident, or like ours through suicide, that should not be who they were. Our children lived a life that was meant to be remembered as a life that gave back to our world."

Andrew and Denise Kappa, in honor of our son, Justin

"Dr. Mary's display of internal reflection expressed honestly the turmoil a parent travels after losing their child(ren) and provides reflections to make the best of the situation and to heal. She shared her journey in hopes that others can see they are not alone on their own journey."

Greg and Toni Hostetler, in honor of our children,
Tania Lee & Joseph Gregory Hostetler

"My journey mirrored many aspects of Dr. Mary's. Digesting the information in the way she shared her story allowed me to reflect on my story, mourn my daughter, Casey, and find hope and inspiration for my future. I would recommend this book to any bereaved parent. Her intuitive approach provides a foundation for self-reflection, self-discovery, and finding a way to honor loved ones and yourself."

Jennie and Bill Reimer, in honor of our daughter,
Casey Reimer

"Life goes on without our loved ones, Dr. Mary provides insights to make the journey more self-reflective and to allow for healing to occur. She bared her soul to help others understand they are not alone in their despair and that they will learn and adapt honoring their child's memories. Thank you for sharing your journey."

Ron and Linda Spadafore in honor of our son,
Nick Spadafore

"*Journey into the Looking Glass* reminds us that what we are feeling is *normal*—and we are not alone in our Journey. This book would be a valuable tool for bereaved parents along with the friends and loved ones of those suffering the loss of a child, to perhaps gain some small understanding of what we are going through."

Julie and Paul Tsatsos, in honor of their sons,
Darryl and Ryan Tsatsos

"Dr. Mary has grasped the pain of loss and allowed us to experience the loss of her daughter, Susie. We lost our precious Rochelle and found the principles of the book to be very intuitive and healing as we remember, reflect, and build our new normal always relating her importance in our lives moving forward."

Tacey and Rebecca Fons, in honor of our precious
Rochelle Zeeman

Other Books by the Author

Dr. Mary Welsh, Author, National Speaker, and Grief Session Facilitator desires to aid those facing adversity and grief with a positive perspective. Consider reading her additional resources:

Journey into the Looking Glass: The Four Aspects of Positive Reflection Journal
- A journal to document your thoughts as you Remember, Reflect, Recreate, and Relate.

Susie Q's Kids Positive Reflections: My Special Angel
- A children's grief book addressing the questions a child may pose after the loss of a loved one.

Susie Q's Kids Positive Reflections: Good Characteristics Coloring Book
- A children's coloring book reflecting on the positive aspects a child should model.

JOURNEY INTO THE LOOKING GLASS

FINDING HOPE AFTER THE LOSS OF LOVED ONES

DR. MARY WELSH

Printed in the United States of America

Published by Author Academy Elite
PO Box 43, Powell, OH 43035
www.AuthorAcademyElite.com

Identifiers:
LCCN: 2019910240
ISBN: 978-1-64085-791-9 (paperback)
ISBN: 978-1-64085-792-6 (hardback)
ISBN: 978-1-64085-793-3 (ebook)

Available in paperback, hardback, e-book, and audiobook.

Any Internet addresses (websites, blogs, etc.) and telephone numbers printed in this book are offered as a resource. They are not intended in any way to be or imply an endorsement by Author Academy Elite, nor does Author Academy Elite vouch for the content of these sites and numbers for the life of this book.

Foreword by Debra Hayes
Cover design by Debbie O'Bryne
Book design by Chris O'Bryne
Editorial review by Marvin Wilmes
Pictorial Illustrators: April L'Ecuyer-dye and Joseph Welsh

DEDICATION

I dedicate this book to my daughter, Susie (Q) McBride-Welsh, who passed away at 31 years of age from septic shock following a series of lifelong illnesses. She is finally pain free.

Her death impacted so many. I also dedicate it to her family and friends. While mourning her death, they brought honor to her by living their lives filled with love, happiness, passion, and purpose, which was her wish for each of them.

As you read the book, remember the song we sang as she left us: "You Are My Sunshine" and realize that she worked hard all her life to be the best she could. "You Got This" now. Live a life full of compassion, love, happiness, joy, empathy, and trust, inspiring others to do the same.

LEAVE A REVIEW

If you found this book relevant, informative, and it helped you on your grief journey, share it with others so others can find comfort, passion, and purpose on their road to self-discovery as they create their new normal. Please help me share the message by adding an Amazon review and a Barnes and Nobles review on their websites. Thank you.

THE FOUR ASPECTS OF POSITIVE REFLECTION

Remember: Understand Your Past and How Your Loved Ones Impacted You–Remember the Good and Bad Memories

Reflect: Understand Your Journey and Path to Grasping the Impact You Had on Your Loved Ones and They Had on You

Recreate: Get in Touch and Come to Grips with Them– Embrace Your New Normal

Relate: Make Your Commitment to Your "New Normal" Give of Yourself for a Better Life–Practice Self-care, Supporting Others, and Giving Back in the Community

The Four Aspects of Positive Reflection

The Power of Positivity

Remember: Understand Your Past and How Your Loved Ones Impacted You–Remember the Good and Bad Memories–Your life has changed forever, and memories will always fill it with a sense of loss for what is missing from your life. It will be your "New Normal."

To understand my approach, I shared some stories about my daughter, Susan McBride-Welsh (Susie Q), and a tribute from her dad, Joseph Welsh. I encourage you to do the same. It provides an anchor for where we came from, the good times, and the well of hope that can feed our injured souls. Although the journey will have ups and downs, by designing a clear picture of our past, it will lead us to a closer destination of hope, inspiration, passion, and purpose. The first step toward getting there is asking for help. This book will define my journey and a potential roadmap of self-discovery to consider your next move.

Reflect: Understand Your Journey and Path to Grasping the Impact You Had on Your Loved Ones and They Had on You–Nothing ever goes exactly according to plan; your journey will take you through the stages of grief in no particular order. The gut-wrenching sorrow can hit you at any time. Understanding the stages are normal may provide you with some techniques to get you through your moments. It is about understanding things are different. We must learn to move forward never forgetting their life and contributions but learning how to live a life without their physical presence. The most crucial aspect is self-care, working through this book is a step in the right direction. Be open, be honest with others, don't be afraid to speak up, to take care of your needs, to say "no," to whatever. It is your journey and thus personal to you and your feelings, practice self-care to get in tune with your feelings.

Recreate: Get in Touch and Come to Grips with Them–Embrace Your New Normal–"What If is a dangerous statement. These "What If" statements can play with our emotions daily as we reminisce about days gone by etched in our memories. We long for the current day vacancies, voids, and hopes as well as the future wishes that will never come true. Learning to cope with them and remembering their loss and your own losses can be daunting as you create your "New Normal." Practice identifying your "What If" statement and replace them with "But I/we Did" statements. This technique challenged my thought patterns to reflect on the positive side of "What If" statements and the actions and relationships that impact my approach to life.

Relate: Make Your Commitment to Your "New Normal" Give of Yourself for a Better Life–Practice Self-care, Supporting Others, and Giving Back in the Community–Loss happens in many different ways and impacts each of us differently. Look at your situation, what you can do, what you can commit to doing, the people in your life to aid you, and the people in your life you need to support. Learn that everyone grieves differently. Devote your actions to make a commitment and impact on growing and healing. Expressing your grief with others makes it more palatable, it allows you to connect and find solace in their relationship with you and enables you to establish guidelines to make life more acceptable and purposeful.

TABLE OF CONTENTS

LIST OF ILLUSTRATIONS

FOREWORD

Debra Hayes - *RISE: What to Do When Hell Won't Back Off and 40 Days to Rise: A Devotional to Build A Life Overcoming Disappointment, Heartache and Tragedy*

JOURNEY INTO THE LOOKING GLASS
by Dr. Mary Welsh

The heart of a grieving parent and the soul of a beautiful caring person is on display throughout *Journey into the Looking Glass*. The unique style of Dr. Mary Welsh not only exposes her emotions as she experiences the loss of her daughter Susie-Q but gives readers a definite plan to help them deal with their losses.

If you felt the need to read *Journey into the Looking Glass* you may find yourself in the unfortunate group that Dr. Mary and I belong. This circle of parents includes many members who have said good-bye to their children entirely too soon. As a mother who has four children who now live in heaven, I heard and felt the hope in every word this author wrote.

Dr. Mary describes the life of Susie-Q in such a vivid way that you feel you knew her by the time you finish the book. The love, sadness, and hope come to life on each page. Following her example may spark creative ways to memorize and express your love for your child.

Dr. Mary and I share the same passion as parents moving forward with an empty heart. We believe that it is such a pivotal time to embrace life again, which does not mean we are lessening the memory of our children. There is a season during and immediately following the loss where you are still in disbelief, and thoughts are foggy. *Journey into the Looking Glass* lets you walk with Dr. Mary through this stage. However, she expresses her mission and passion as she shares with you powerful revelations and easy steps to help you start walking forward again. She understands the devastating effect grief can have on a person if it settles in and tries to define your life.

Walk with Dr. Mary and Susie-Q through their *Journey into the Looking Glass*. I am confident you will find the compassion, reflection, and encouragement to continue on your journey and engage in your own life again.

Debra Lynn Hayes
Best Selling Author, Speaker and Coach
RISE: What to Do When Hell Won't Back Off
40 Days to Rise: A Devotional to Build A Life Overcoming Disappointment, Heartache and Tragedy.
DebraLynnHayes.com

Endorsed by Best Selling Authors

❖ Lisa Boehm - *Journey to HEALING: A Mother's Guide to Navigating Child Loss*

❖ Laura Diehl - Award-winning author of several books, including *When Tragedy Strikes*

❖ Melanie DeLorme – *After the Flowers Die: A Handbook of Heartache, Hope and Healing After Losing a Child*

❖ Marvin Wilmes, *Beyond the Horizon: Crisis of Faith* and *Chronicles: Journey toward Hope, Overcoming Loss through Faith, Perseverance, and Surrender*

❖ Kary Oberbrunner, author of *Your Secret Name and Elixir Project*

PREFACE

What precipitated my writing this book? My young daughter, Susan McBride-Welsh (Susie Q), passed away from septic shock at the age of thirty-one. She suffered most of her adult life with one condition or another riddled with pain but always addressed life with positivity and a smile. Her unconditional love of life aided her in leading a life full of love, laughter, and caring for others.

Susie had a surgery that never fully healed, and the infection stemming from the area spread through her bloodstream, aggressively taking her from us. Since she was ill and had skirted death in the past, in our numerous discussions she was adamant in her wishes for no extreme measures. When the doctors said she was terminally ill, the decision was easy because of her desires—we let her go on her next journey with love. It broke our hearts; our angel soared without pain.

Utilize this book as your passport on your journey to finding your new normal. Use it as a Roadmap of Self-Help and Discovery. This book describes the impact Susie Q's journey through life had on her family and friends. Her journey beyond had a profound effect on each of us and others in our community. Please understand I am writing this during the most traumatic time of my life. I am basing it on my personal experiences, observations, and beliefs. I had discussions with others to help review my thoughts, assumptions, and approach to grieving; I am a consultant and professor and not a medical professional. Therefore, my approach is not grounded in medical theory but from the heartfelt emotional foundation of a grieving mother and her family and friends.

LIST OF ABBREVIATIONS

AAE – Authors Academy Elite

AFSP – American Foundation of Suicide Prevention

SHRM – Society of Human Resources

TAPS -Tragedy Assistance Program for Survivors of fallen
military members

LIST OF CONTRIBUTORS

Throughout my journey, I was very fortunate to have my husband and soulmate Joseph Welsh by my side every step of the way. His strength supported our family and me as we made the necessary decisions and tried to function and find a new normal. As my best friend, he listened when I needed to talk, cry, scream, or rant at the injustice of it all.

I wrote down my thoughts, and he inspired me to write this book and start our non-profit, Susie Q's Kids. His true friendship was the catalyst for my writing and speaking about my struggles and commitment to aid other adults grieving and to brighten and inspire the lives of children and young adults through the distribution of our comfort bags.

I am eternally grateful God blessed me with my beautiful Angel Susie and her siblings. Angela McBride is her big sister, her confidante, her protector, her everything. Her positive attitude and unwavering philosophy that her sister is always with us made life more comfortable. Through our stories and travels, Susie continues to live on as an active member of our family.

James McBride, and Susie's big brother, was always her hero. Her heart had stopped seven years before her death. Jim performed CPR, and we were blessed with her existence for another seven years. She called him her super-hero. His quiet demeanor of support and strength allowed his immediate family to heal and has been a source of strength for me. His wife Karly, children (Brandon, Jakob, and Luke), and himself surround me with joy and bring life to our days and hope to our future. Nana and Papa's love blossoms in their presence.

Shawna, Chris, and the girls Ella and Clara bring comfort with their visits from out-of-state, their constant phone calls, pictures, and warm words. Susie's last trip was to visit them in Minnesota. Nana and Papa enjoy every visit and relish in the love that surrounds us.

Ashley, Dusty, and Vicki brought understanding, watching over our every need in the home, dealing with the mundane functions of living in the beginning, and always being supportive. Their commitment and love did not go unnoticed, and their crazy antics will warm our hearts for many a day. Step-sister Jodi brought love and joy to her life.

To my mom Shirley Morgan, thank you for your love and for being a role model throughout our lives. We can always overcome adversity. You love us, unconditionally. You let us know we are able to succeed at whatever we put our minds to, even if it is unthinkable like the loss of our child. Your ability to adapt has always instilled in me a strength to keep going. You are amazing! Thank you, mom.

To our parents, Shirley Morgan and Judy and Basil Welsh, our mutual consideration for each other, your kind words of encouragement, and our need to share stories enabled me to write and capture the essence of Susie and her impact and the path our family took to heal healthily. Thank you for your never-ending love and support. You were an inspirational part of Susie's life and continue to instill love, compassion, and purpose in our daily lives.

To April for being Susie's best friend, a friend to the entire family, and for her passion and empathy as we revisited all of the pictures from Susie's life to locate the best ones for the book and to reflect on them and the stories shared throughout this book with laughter and tears. You helped me heal reliving those moments together, thank you.

To our family, our siblings, their kids, extended family members, thanks for being there for Susie in life and surrounding us with love following her passing. For those that got the panicked phone call or visits, thanks for keeping me from the despair of the dark rabbit hole of grief and self-pity. Your ability to make me smile and laugh at good memories kept me going.

I cherish our friends, old and new. You were willing to let me share and talk about the loss of Susie. Your support continues to mean so much to me. To those that have lost a child, my heart breaks for you and your loss, I find comfort that our angels are together watching over us. May we all find peace on our new paths of self-discovery and healing.

To the professionals that provided support, guidance, and talked me through my grieving process, I am indebted to JF and KT for your time, compassion, and understanding as I traveled the different stages of grieving and healing. Your encouragement made this book a reality and will hopefully aid other readers traveling along their journey and path to healing.

I must also recognize Dr. C, Dr. F, Dr. K, Dr. Z and Wes for the care, support, and guidance they extended Susie in life, she always appreciated your time, care, friendship, and guidance.

Fr. Richard Welsh, thank you for your spiritual guidance, love, support, and the beautiful words as Susan found peace.

Finally, to the authors who shared their stories and insights, the Author Academy Elite (AAE) and Business

Academy Elite (BAE) support team, the AAE Guild editors, and my beta reader Donna Mirabito; thank you for your insights to make my story more impactful and available to those in need. I hope this book and online resources act as a Passport for Self-Discovery, providing insights and guidance to others. May they find hope following the loss of their loved ones as they reflect on their *Journey into the Looking Glass.*

FOUR ASPECTS OF POSITIVE REFLECTION

Remember: Understand Your Past and How Your Loved Ones Impacted You–Remember the Good and Bad Memories

Reflect: Understand Your Journey and Path to Grasping the Impact You Had on Your Loved Ones and They Had on You

Recreate: Get in Touch and Come to Grips with Them–Embrace Your New Normal

Relate: Make Your Commitment to Your "New Normal" Give of Yourself for a Better Life–Practice Self-care, Supporting Others, and Giving Back in the Community

The Four Aspects of Positive Reflection

The Power of Positivity

Journey into the Looking Glass

Finding Hope after the Loss of Loved Ones

Dr. Mary Welsh

ONE
WHO WAS SUSIE Q?

SHORT STORIES

Susie Q was a miracle from the beginning. I miscarried three children, and she had two older siblings, her brother, Jim, and sister, Angela. They said I would lose her at seventeen weeks, but after a maternity cycle of bedrest, she was born. She had health issues from the start, and the worst materialized in her young adult life.

I wish to remember her with laughter, so I will share a few special memories that bring a smile to my face.

It's My Party

As a young girl, she felt her friends liked her sister Angela better. One birthday she was crying under the kitchen table because she thought her friends liked her sister better. My response was to sing, "It's my party, and I'll cry if I want to…" The song always made her smile thinking of that incident as her sister is her best friend.

Molester Van

When she was in second or third grade, there were episodes where the school sent notices home about "stranger danger." One day walking home from school (1 ½ blocks), a white cargo van (she called them molester vans) crept slowly down the street behind her. She panicked and ran to the porch of a house on the block. Her horror increased as the van pulled in the driveway, and the man got out of the car and asked, "if she needed help." It was his house and she ran away screaming in terror—poor kid.

Troll Doll

Her brother Jim liked to tease her. We had a full-size van, the Purple Barney Mobile, and he would place her troll dolls on top of it out of reach and watch her try to jump to retrieve them. Oh, how silly, they were the best of friends throughout their lives.

Hillbilly

Her father's family is from Tennessee. When Susie was little, I always said she was part hillbilly. She was mad that the teacher and class laughed at her when she proudly stood up in the front of the class and said she was "French, German, Irish, and hillbilly." The teacher had her say it twice. I almost wrote it on her death certificate, my silly little hillbilly.

Camping

She loved to go camping with our family and friends and with her friends and their families. She loved all aspects of camping: S'mores, hobo pies, campfires, hikes, swimming, and water balloon fights. She could set up and tear down the popup camper like a pro. Campers shared many a fun story around those campfires of cherished memories.

Gramma Visit

Susie loved to feel special. I had to have surgery, and she got to stay with gramma and grampa up north while her siblings were at camp. She went to the library and read several books every day, rode in the golf cart on the property, and learned the names of all the birds. It was a treat she and her grandmother talked about often, even got a book of birds as a souvenir.

Don't Mess with My Girl

Her friend April was her school protector. In grade school, Susie carried a bit of extra weight, and the kids could be cruel. April put those offenders in their place: no one messed with Susie! They were each other's protectors throughout every stage of their lives.

Driver Permit and the Cat Allergy

Susie wanted to see her gramma for a week-long visit. She drove up to my sister's home a half-hour away from gramma's. Not thinking that my sister's cats would set off my allergies, my eyes, unfortunately, swelled shut. Susie had to forgo her vacation with gramma and drive me downstate since I literally could not open my eyes. She had her driver's permit. I said if she got pulled over, I would pry my eyes open. She laughed when she got home. We made it in record time: I couldn't see the speedometer, and she took full advantage of the situation—my little speed demon.

Uni

We were camping on Susie's birthday when she turned sixteen. She insisted on going to the Secretary of State office to get her driver's license and on driving her car (nicknamed Uni) for the rest of the visit. Oh, the planning and joy of getting to drive. She couldn't wait until we got home, she was so excited.

Pool Days

Susie loved to hang out by the pools with her siblings, cousins, friends, and aunts, as there are always some fun times under the sun with laughter and an abundance of good food. The nighttime had bonfires. Flowers surround the yard.

Susie has left her mark in the garden and celebrates all our occasions with us.

Mustang

I took Susie to the dealership to buy a new car, and they wouldn't let her test drive it due to her age. I signed the papers and had to go back to work, so I threw Susie the keys and said drop me off and pick me up at 5 p.m. She picked up her friend April for the first ride. The car stayed in the family until the engine blew years later. Her friends April and Dave (a mechanic) restored it, and the vehicle has a "Susie Q" license plate in honor of her. Susie would be happy they own it. It's still in the family.

Door Wall

During a family gathering by the pool, Susie was lying on the couch sick, just talking to people coming and going through the family room. Uncle Jim had a plate of food, and he thought the door wall was open. "Whomp." The plate hit his chest. Susie's laughter was contagious. Whenever she would start laughing for no apparent reason, she would say, "I just thought of Uncle Jim and the door wall."

Valparaiso

Susie and her friends loved visiting her brother Jim and his friends at college. She loved hanging with her brother and his fraternity friends. She became everyone's little sister.

Lollapalooza and Concerts

She loved to go to concerts with her sister Angela, a fashion designer and stylist. She enjoyed the music, the atmosphere, the friends, but mostly hanging out with her sister and assisting with her jobs with performers, concerts, tours, videos, and commercials. She loved seeing life through her sister's eyes and feeling the music.

Bonfires

She loved talking and hanging out around a campfire at our home, at cousins Cheryl and Jamie's houses, and at the campgrounds. Many a funny antic and story went on around the fire.

Comedy Show – Laughter

Susie loved comedy. We watched "Last Comic Standing" and other comedy shows, attended comedy shows and open mic shows. During one show, she was laughing so hard the comedian stopped, looked to the balcony, and said, "this is going to be easier than I thought," as she was doubled over laughing. Laughter is good medicine.

Vegas, Miss USA, Broken Foot

Angela and Susie's friend Channing who was Miss Michigan, traveled to Las Vegas for the Miss USA pageant. Susie didn't tell the girls until the trip home that she had broken her foot the first night. She was bound and determined to have a good time, and she certainly did.

Nephews, Nieces and Friends' Kids

She was always willing to go the extra mile with kids: Dave & Buster's, Chuck E. Cheese's, the apple orchards, pumpkin patches, parks, the zoo, birthday celebrations, trick-or-treating, sporting events, Jungle Java, eateries, water parks, and holidays. You could always hear her enjoying the kids at home, making cookies and crafts, by the pool, or out and about. All the kids loved time with Aunt Susie, and she loved them. One visit on a giant slide while holding the kids, her tiny butt airlifted, the look on her face, the tight hold, and then the laughter, are a good memory. Brandon, Jakob, Luke, Ella and Clara, Katie, and Sarah—Aunt Susie loves you.

Cousins

Susie interchanged the words cousins with siblings, more like brothers and sisters. Anyone lucky enough to be part of the family whether biological, officially related by law, or by friendship, they felt a close kinship. Cousins Lisa, Jamie, Cheryl, Jack, Leslie, Clay, Doug, Rachel, Jason, Lindsay, TJ, Tucker, Mallory, Carlene, Jack, Christina, Cindy, Joshua, Jeremy, Jocelyn, Jacob, Jessica, Sarah, Ryan, and Paige, thanks for all the stories and memories you and your partners and families shared. Camping, fashion shows, making cookies and crafts, vacations, pool days, sleepovers, sports—lots of laughter! You are loved beyond measure. Remember her fondly in the antics you each shared, the bonds you formed, and the joy you brought each other.

Aunts and Uncles

Susie felt a part of each family unit, she jokingly said she was the favorite intertwined in each of your lives. She was comfortable to stay awhile, share a story, laugh with and at you, swim, boat, put together a puzzle, and visit a park or zoo. She shared special moments with you all, remember them with a smile as she enjoyed each of you and being a part of our crazy family. A special shout out to second mommies Aunt Carol and Aunt Pam.

Giving

Susie was always the champion for good and for those less fortunate. She rang the bell for the Salvation Army, wrapped presents for Cops for Kids, took up collections for those who suffered a fire or a personal setback, participated in bake sales, fundraising, and food drives. Ask, and she would give it to you or find a way to get the help—she made a difference in the lives of others, and her legacy continues with our non-profit, Susie Q's Kids, brightening and inspiring the lives of children and young adults "one comfort bag at a time".

Hospital Living

Susie was in and out of the hospital for much of her life. She was always thankful for the care that the medical assistants, techs, transporters, nurses, and physicians provided. She loved the comfort dogs that visited as she adored her two dogs (Hershey and Abby, who are with her in heaven). She would wear her Detroit Lions gear on game day and shout at the TV, sing the fight song, and trash-talk me by text if I was at the game.

She colored pictures with the staff and decorated her hospital room with them. Although she hurt, Susie tried to maintain her smiles, thank everyone, and offer them goodies and laughter when they entered her room. She was appreciative of the care she received, as evidenced in the picture with Nurse Kelsey. Susie was a precious soul so full of life and caring!

Her Funeral

Susie was laid out at the funeral home for one day. More than 500 people came to pay their respects. The stories I heard, the messages shared, the laughter in the room as her three year old nieces and nephews would stop to stroke her arm and say they loved her, to the next person telling me they were a friend, a work associate, a patient, a nurse or physician, or family. You didn't need to be a blood relation to be family. You were just accepted.

I had remarried, and Susie called my husband, Joe, her MOD (My Other Dad), and his daughters, Dusty, Shawna, and Ashley, her sisters. One day shortly before she died, Susie asked Joe to legally adopt her at age thirty-one. Unfortunately, she had not completed the legal paperwork, but she is and always will be both of ours: Susie McBride-Welsh.

Her wake was filled with picture boards from her young life with her siblings Jim and Angela, family, and friends. A picture without a smile could not be found among them. We will forever remember Susie for her spirit, her good nature, big heart, and love of us and of life!

Susan Renee McBride-Welsh (Susie Q)

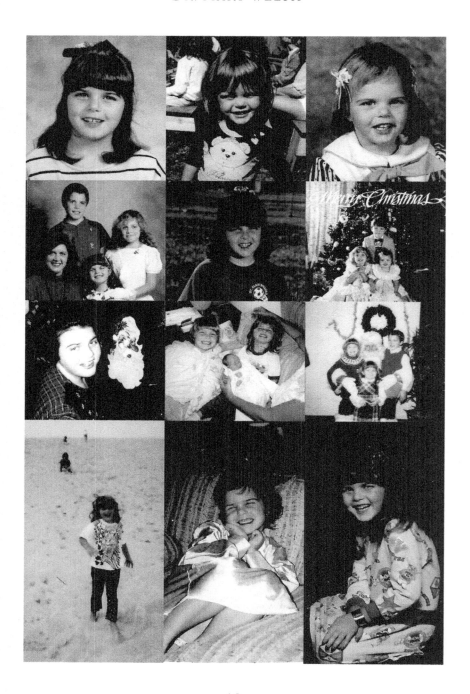

Roadmap to Self Help and Discovery Key Takeaways:

❖ Memories are precious, preserve them.
❖ Let other's share their memories, capture them.
❖ The healing starts when we can look back and smile remembering these treasures.

Express your emotions:
What precious stories do you remember? What does your family and friends remember and share? What videos, text messages, voice messages, and pictures can you capture to keep those precious memories alive? How will you retain them: electronic storage, teddy bears with audio, scrapbooks, jewelry, etc. Make a list to capture your thoughts and others.

_____

_____

_____

_____

_____

_____

What is your action plan?

_____

_____

_____

TWO

DAD'S TRIBUTE

Susie Q.

Driving in my car, I am wondering what I will write. I always think about you as I drive to and from work. There are times that I talk to you for the whole ride. There are times that I cannot help but cry because I miss you so much. Some days seem so long since you've left. Some of them are hard to get through, but I know I can never give up because you never did. I know I will see you again someday, and we will share all the memories and emotions when we see each other again.

Why did you have to leave so soon? Why did you have to go? These are two questions I constantly ask almost every day. I may never know the answers to these questions, but I will never stop asking them. I know that you are in heaven with all our other relatives and friends watching down on us. I know that you are no longer in pain and I rejoice in that. We now carry a pain that is ours because we love you so much and miss you. It is a different kind of pain, but we will carry it with the strength and courage that you had carried yours.

Some days are worse than others. The pain of missing you overwhelms us, and we can hardly do anything. On those days we take some time to miss you and remember you, and we come out of the tailspin and move forward. I know that you will be waiting for us when it is our time to leave this life. I look forward to being reunited with you and getting one of your loving hugs. I miss those so much.

As a parent, we hope that our kids learn from the lessons that we show them. I know that you exhibited a lot of the values that you had learned from us and others in your life. I also have the honor of learning some lessons from you. You have taught me many lessons while watching you battle your medical conditions. One of them is that it costs us nothing to say hello to someone, even if they are a stranger. It costs us nothing, but it might mean a million bucks to the person you are greeting. Another lesson I learned was to be strong and face your issues head on and find a solution to them instead of asking, why me?

You and your sisters and brother are my guiding light. The six of you will guide me on my path going forward. I hold all our memories even tighter these days now that I know that tomorrows are not guaranteed. I will follow my road forward until we are reunited once again. When I see you again, I will rejoice in your spirit, and hug you, and will not want to let you go. I will be happy and sad when all this happens. I will be happy to be reunited with you and all the others who have left before me, but sad to leave behind all those who must continue their journey.

Love and miss you with all my heart, Dad (Joseph Welsh).

You Are My Sunshine!

Roadmap to Self Help and Discovery Key Takeaways:

- ❖ Music affects people differently, find comfort in the lyrics, the meaning, the musicality of the song, and the memory or feelings it brings forth within you.
- ❖ Play it often either for personal or public listening, bond with your loved ones and the feelings it invokes.
- ❖ The healing occurs as we embrace them in our "new normal" always remembering the treasure of their impact on our past, present, and future until we see them again.

Express your emotions:

What song(s) resonate with you? What precious stories and memories do you remember? Take your pictures and make a video including the music for your own listening pleasure. Find a way to honor them, find some measure of peace in the lyrics of the song, embrace the thoughts that make you smile remembering them, their impact, and the knowledge you will see them again!

_____

_____

_____

What is your action plan?

_____

_____

THREE
DISCOVER YOUR NEW YOU –
YOU GOT THIS!

How is it possible to move on?
Why does life feel so empty and
lonely without you?

My loved ones surround me,
my family and friends, but so alone!

How do I overcome the challenge of
living this new norm?
I miss my daughter and the old me.

How do I ensure family and friends
understand how important she was?
Still is to each of us?

Will people forget her?
Will her memories fade?
Will she become a distant memory
or thought?

I talk about her all the time.
It is my way of grieving and living.
It permits others to talk.

By speaking about her, I remember the way she lived,
the aspirations she had,
the impact she had on others, and how
I can embrace those memories and hopes.

In writing, I tell her story and mine.
My wish is to provide some glimmer of hope to
each of us who may have lost a loved one!

By volunteering and starting Susie Q's Kids,
a nonprofit in her honor,
I can continue to share her story,
heal in a healthy manner,
provide family and friends with an avenue to
heal, and most importantly,
brighten and inspire the lives of children and
young adults with our comfort bags.
She would love this, that thought gives me
Peace and Purpose.

As we celebrate birthdays, births, graduations,
holidays, and special moments,
remember them fondly,
listen to your heart as you may have a
"moment, where you are overwhelmed
by their loss," but think of
how they would handle the situation,
how they lived,
how their thirst for life warmed your heart,
gave them peace, made them laugh and

made you proud and
happy to be in their lives.
They are with us every moment of every day.
Feel their presence.

It is important to appreciate them,
to acknowledge their loss, our grief,
our longing to hold them,
to tell them "we love you,"
to share that laugh, kudos, tears, gratitude, and
how proud we were to have been a part of
their life's journey as their loved one.

Keep them alive in your mind and heart,
acknowledge your new you, and
how devastated you are by their absence.

Take it day by day, hour by hour, and
minute by minute. I write this following the
second Thanksgiving without my girl.

We put our Christmas tree up with
our grandchild today. He was so excited.
Everything seems normal but so surreal,
the boxes of personal ornaments from
a lifetime of holidays boxed away in the basement,
a new tree with new bulbs adorns the room.

The wounds too fresh to open the boxes and
relive those precious memories that
might take me down the rabbit hole, that
dark place of despair.

Do what is best for you; ask for help,
seek counseling, and start new traditions.
Whatever it takes to avoid the rabbit hole.

Instead of the fun-filled day of laughter and
promises for the future, picking up blankets and
items for our nonprofit replaces the
Black Friday shopping tradition.

We will continue to help others
through our nonprofit efforts.
We hope to brighten the lives of other
children and their families, finding happiness in
enriching their lives. We care.

The thought of another holiday without her is
so frustrating, devastating, and heart-wrenching.
How will we do it?

Each of us must cope in our own way.
Mine will be to surround myself with others and
ask them to speak of her, to share their memories,
to remind me that her life mattered, and
to create new memories.

She was able to overcome so much in
her lifetime.
I can hear her say this and mean it,
"You Are Amazing. You Got This!"

Embrace this new normal, do what is best for you,
what honors your loved one's memory,
whatever gets you through the moment,

the hour, the day, or the minute.
Your loved one would want the best for you.

Can you hear them telling you
to live life to its fullest?
You Are Amazing. You Got This!

FIND AND EMBRACE YOUR NEW NORMAL.

Roadmap to Self Help and Discovery Key Takeaways:
❖ List what was important to your loved one.
❖ List what they liked to do with you and others and how they shared their feelings.
❖ List the activities that they contributed to or were involved with, create some action items to find some ways to devote your time to as part of your new normal.

Express your emotions:
What kind of comfort do you gain from reflecting on what was important to your loved one? How can you use the information you gathered to create action items to continue to support what was important to them as part of your new normal? Create your own action list.

_____

_____

_____

_____

_____

What is your action plan?

_____

_____

_____

28

FOUR
THE STAGES OF GRIEF

Death is unavoidable. Unfathomable. Indescribable. We each learn to address it in our own style, based on our emotions, and for many of us, on our spiritual beliefs.

Since my daughter's death, I journeyed through the recognized stages of grief. They happen in no particular order. They can occur all at once. But once you can recognize them, it becomes easier to cope with the array of emotions that overwhelm you: crying, ranting, rejoicing, laughing, and coming to terms with your new normal.

The person you lost had a significant impact on you.

> "THERE'S NO TRAGEDY IN LIFE LIKE THE DEATH OF A CHILD. THINGS NEVER GET BACK TO THE WAY THEY WERE." (DWIGHT D. EISENHOWER, N.D.).[1]

Understanding that the loss has impacted you will help you come to terms with the fact that you will never be the same. You will need to come to terms with your new normal as there is a void, a chasm of loss, despair, guilt, and what-ifs that will cause you to pause.

STAGES OF GRIEF

According to Recover from Grief.com, they identify "the seven stages of grief as:

(1) shock and denial
(2) pain and guilt
(3) anger and bargaining
(4) depression, reflection, and loneliness
(5) the upward turn
(6) reconstruction and working through, and
(7) acceptance and hope." [2]

These stages can provide insights into our loss. I say Susie's name often to keep her alive in my mind. I encourage others to talk about Susie freely and to celebrate her life and the impact she had on theirs. Although speaking of Susie may invoke any or all of these grief stages, it is a healthy way of channeling the grief and the loss. Speaking of your loved one is a way of developing our new existence, your new you, your new normal, as life has forever changed. The past is full of memories and our future is yet to be defined, but how we approach each day will enable us to deal with the changes that life brings us. Thus, wherever I state Susie or my daughter, say your loved one's name or relationship.

Each of these stages happens. There is no specific time-frame and it has no linear meaning. The stages do not happen in any particular order and can happen at any time. A picture, a memory, a visitor, a special outing, a special celebration, a book, movie, or song, a birthday, a quiet moment, a walk in the park—just about anything can spark a memory, and the grief can hit you full force at that moment. How we react will enable us to move forward, to remember with a smile, a sense of loss, a laugh, a tear, a shared hug, or a recounting of shared memories.

My stories will provide insights into how I have handled the situation and will provide you with the ability to see that you are not alone on your grief journey. Many have traveled the path. Learning from others on how they survived their losses may provide you with a feeling of hope, that what you are feeling is normal, and that life will continue as your new normal unveils.

> "ONLY PEOPLE WHO ARE CAPABLE OF LOVING STRONGLY CAN ALSO SUFFER GREAT SORROW, BUT THIS SAME NECESSITY OF LOVING SERVES TO COUNTERACT THEIR GRIEF AND HEALS THEM." (LEO TOLSTOY, N.D.).[3]

1) SHOCK AND DENIAL

> Regardless of the situation, we are never really prepared to hear that our loved ones are gone. The moment is incomprehensible, so much so, that we cannot wrap our heads around it. You will probably react to learning of the loss with numbed disbelief. You may deny the reality of the loss at some level in order to avoid the pain. Shock provides the emotional protection from being overwhelmed all at once. This may last for weeks. [4]

Because my daughter had been ill her entire adult life, in and out of hospitals and in constant pain, we had discussed her wishes regarding life and death. She promised never to take her own life, although she admitted that she hurt so much that it had crossed her mind. She promised me because I had stated, "If you take your own life, I will always wonder if I missed something or if I could have done something to prevent it. If the Lord takes you, I will be sad, but know you are in good hands."

Those who succumb to suicide, in my opinion, are not in their rational minds. Overwhelmed by the situation and despair in their existence, they believe others are better off without them or having to care for them. Don't blame them. They are not thinking clearly and rationally. Have the discussions with others to let them know you are there, that help is available, and they are never a burden. You may be saving their life or someone they know by discussing this often-taboo subject. You may also prevent others from experiencing the grief of their loss.

When the doctors said that Susie would never be off the ventilator, her organs were shutting down, and she would not regain consciousness, my decision was easy. I remembered each surgery where she would call and talk to her family members while in pre-op, and I would see her taken away with tears in her eyes hearing her telling the nurses, "I have a DNR (Do Not Resuscitate) order." It broke my heart every time! She had so many plans, so many friends; she didn't want to die, but she never wanted to live on machines or be a burden to her family. She had seen this and was adamant that she did not want to live that way.

When the Intensive Care Unit (ICU) doctors said she was critically ill, I said she had a DNR order. Her sister said, "don't kill her, momma," and her brother uttered a simple, "Oh, no!" Others looked on in shock and denial and cried, praying for a miracle. Susie had overcome so much; she would be OK. But not this time.

While the doctors performed tests, it provided us the opportunity to say goodbye. When the results said her organs were shutting down, we surrounded her bed, said our prayers, and sang "You Are My Sunshine."

We (her mom, dad, sister, and one of her aunts) stayed in the room when she took her last breath. She was so peaceful, and her essence infused us all. She was finally in no pain! She would forever be with us, but on a different level and in a different form.

Now to deal with the shock and denial. If I had brought Susie to the hospital earlier, the what-ifs are so frustrating. They challenge you to the core, making you wish for one more minute, one more hug, one more opportunity to say goodbye or I love you, one more time. The "what- ifs" and the "one-mores" drive you crazy! Not only yours but those of your loved ones. We left her in good hands at the hospital, went directly to the funeral home, completed the arrangements, and returned home numb from the whole experience.

We always have a full house, as it's the meeting place for our large family. We decided to have her funeral on her grandfather's birthday. It was only fitting, as they were both angels and it gave me some sense of comfort to know she was with my daddy. The shock and denial of the situation brought us together. People came and brought food. They brought pictures and told stories. They reminisced as I walked around in a fog, not believing she was gone. The busy atmosphere kept people talking, laughing, crying, and reminiscing. They created 42 picture boards for the funeral—a funeral home record. In each picture, from a baby up to the time she passed, Susie was smiling and laughing. She is still smiling as an angel, no doubt as she is pain-free. Those smiles haunt me as I would love to hug her just one more time.

Roadmap to Self Help and Discovery Key Takeaways:
- ❖ The brain fog helps protect you from the indescribable pain of loss.
- ❖ Let others surround you and care for you; it is their way of helping.
- ❖ There is no right or wrong way to react, don't feel you must act a certain way.

Express your emotions:
Give yourself a break; the fog is real. What can you do to help yourself: make lists, journal, calendars, etc.? What was/is your story? What helped you before/after? What was your reaction? Who is(are) your go to person(s)? When you need help, contact them.

_____

_____

_____

_____

_____

What is your action plan?

_____

_____

_____

2) PAIN AND GUILT:

The pain and guilt can be physically felt. Your body and mind are racked with the "what ifs," the "should haves," the "could haves," and the "whys" racing through your mind, body, heart, and soul.

As the shock wears off, it is replaced with the suffering of unbelievable pain. Although excruciating and almost unbearable, it is important that you experience the pain fully and not hide, avoid, or escape it with alcohol or drugs. You may feel guilty or remorse over things you did or didn't do with your loved one. Life feels chaotic and scary during this phase. [5]

My guilt, it nearly tore me apart thinking of those "what-ifs." If I had done this, would the outcome have been different? I couldn't sleep since nights were our time together. We talked as I graded papers, and she suffered in her moments of pain. Night was my special time with her besides the days, nights, and months in the hospital.

Mornings were her dad's as she would watch for him to walk past her room going to work just to say, "I love you, dad, have a great day." One day he left while Susie was in the bathroom and she was so upset she missed him. Another day before her passing, Susie asked him to adopt her as an adult (she was so excited that he said yes and he that she honored him so). We just had not completed the process. A real regret, but he knows her thoughts and appreciates the fact she did. Daddy Joe!

Knowing that everyone watched me closely, attending to my every need and hurting as much as I was simply could not prevent those heart-wrenching tears from flowing. They came often and I bared my soul, my despair reflected my devastating loss.

People cleaned my house, brought food, and fed me. At times, it felt as if I was removed from the situation. My family physician JF kindly listened and offered me support when I sought medical advice. I tried psychological therapy and my therapist KT was a true treasure as she helped me channel my thoughts.

My husband and I joined Bereaved Parents of USA, Macomb County Chapter, to learn to cope with the pain of our loss and the guilt. Thanks to those members who listened and cried with us as we all looked for that "new normal" without our children.

Roadmap to Self Help and Discovery Key Takeaways:
- ❖ Let your feelings out: laugh, cry, yell, whatever it takes.
- ❖ Realize others hurt as well but want to help; let them as it helps them and you.
- ❖ Seek guidance from medical professionals, we all need help occasionally.

Express your emotions:
What was your reaction? What do you feel guilty about? What are your coping mechanisms? Take stock of behaviors not in your best interests (drinking, smoking, drugs) and how to avoid them. Who can you turn to for support to avoid this type of reaction?

_____

_____

_____

_____

_____

_____

What is your action plan?

_____

_____

_____

3) ANGER AND BARGAINING

Anger that it involves your loved ones can bring forth a plethora of feelings and negotiations with your higher being to try to save them, a futile effort to change the inevitable.

> Frustration gives way to anger, and you may lash out and lay unwanted blame for the death on someone else. Please try to control this, as permanent damage to your relationships may result. This is a time for the release of bottled up emotion. You may rail against fate, questioning, "Why me?" You may also try to bargain in vain with the powers that be for a way out of your despair ('I will never drink again if you just bring him/her back.'). [6]

Why my girl? Why did she experience so much pain? Why? Why? Why? The anger can be consuming and can overtake you if you don't remember the good times.

In my despair, I looked for cards, messages, text messages, emails, Facebook messages, pictures, and mementos to validate our time together. The pain of looking at them brought chasms of pain and anger, taking me to a place of extreme pain as those cherished moments reflected in my brain. But others validated the great relationship we had and how much we meant to each other. The notes and voice messages: "I love you mom." "You are amazing mom; I want to be just like you." "You are the best, I'm so proud of you, have a great time at the Lions game." "You are beautiful." "I love you to the moon and back …"

I JUST WANT HER BACK!

I want to tell Susie how much she meant to me. I know she knew but I want to tell her again, to hug and kiss her again, be with her, and I can't. It sucks but she knows, she always knew. She was my mini-me. We were to grow old together.

The anger is for all the future regrets, those moments when she should have love in her eyes as she buys a home, gets married, has children, gets a new job, takes a vacation, plays "best auntie" with her kiddos, goes to concerts with her sisters, confides in her brother, comforts her grandparents, and enjoys time with her mommy and daddy.

I get angry every time I realize Susie should be here, but now I realize she still is. Her presence surrounds me.

Be receptive. It brings such comfort!

Recently some of her sisters Angie, Karly, and Sammy, went to a concert, each wearing Susie around their necks. They sent me a picture of them holding her sunshine picture to let me know it wouldn't be a concert without her. Susie was with them!

The same day, her gramma had surgery. In the recovery room, she told me that Susie had talked to her and was with her. She was never alone. The surgery was a success. Gramma Shirley found such peace from knowing she was with Susie and talked with her.

Gramma Judy needed surgery twice and had the same response. She knew everything was going to be all right because Susie had spoken to her and laid her hands on her.

Her sister Karly needed surgery. Susie appeared in my dream standing by her bedside, smiling with her thumbs up, meaning "Go for it!" Her surgeries were a success.

We share so many stories of how Susie brings comfort, love, and support to each of us. These stories help to battle my anger at her passing. My fears and pain that life would continue without her are made better knowing that she is never far from any of us—only a thought away!

Roadmap to Self Help and Discovery Key Takeaways:

- ❖ It is normal to be mad, angry, rant, and rally at the injustice of the situation.
- ❖ Remember your loved one is with you, in your memories, your presence, be receptive to signs, and find comfort in them.
- ❖ How do you bargain? How can you be more positive in your actions and reactions?

Express your emotions:

How does anger affect you and others? How did you or can you channel it more positively? What validates your loved one is still with you and others, be receptive to signs they may send? Make note of signs you receive.

_____

_____

_____

_____

_____

What is your action plan?

_____

_____

_____

4) DEPRESSION, REFLECTION, AND LONELINESS

There is no set period for grieving. The pain of the loss of your loved ones can be sparked by a memory, an event, the emptiness of their involvement in your life, the pain of others, and the haunting what-ifs of future events (a wedding, births, grandchild, vacation).

> Just when your friends may think you should be getting on with your life, a long period of sad reflection will likely overtake you. This is a normal stage of grief, so do not be "talked out of it" by well-meaning outsiders. Encouragement from others is not helpful to you during this stage of grieving. During this time, you finally realize the true magnitude of your loss, and it depresses you. You may isolate yourself on purpose, reflect on things you did with your lost one, and focus on memories of the past. You may sense a feeling of emptiness and despair. [7]

I had to get some help from my physician JF, who prescribed a depression medicine and a sleeping aid because I was uncontrollably depressed. The tears came freely. I was overwhelmed with the loss that my baby was gone. Because she had been ill, I spent many days listening to her dreams, her fears, and her feelings (happy and sad). I rubbed her forehead, her back, and her legs, just comforting her. I was her medical advocate. I wiped her tears of pain, frustration, and sense of loss at what her life was now. She just wanted a normal existence but cherished everything she had, everyone she knew, her family, her friends, her thirst for life, helping others, and making a difference.

She wanted to be a full body organ donor, but due to her illness, they couldn't accommodate her wishes. My heart broke when they said they couldn't because the infection had ravaged her body and all they could use was her pacemaker for research. Dazed, I said, "Give it to her brother." In my mind, I relived her experience seven years earlier where her brother, Jim, found her unresponsive and performed CPR, saving her. He was and always will be her hero.

The doctor and my husband looked at me like I was nuts. "OK, sorry, he doesn't need her pacemaker—use it for research." That was the craziness of my shock and wanting to keep some part of her alive.

Talk to your loved ones. What are their wishes regarding life support and organ donation?

ACCORDING TO SUSIE, MY BROTHER IS MY SUPER HERO.

My doctor, my therapist, my support group, my husband, my family, and my friends (new and old) kept me from falling into the abyss of depression. They allowed me to talk freely, to share my thoughts, my tears, my frustrations, my hurt—anything and everything.

They also allowed me to grieve privately. If I was talking and crying in what I called "having a moment," they learned to let me be until I regained my composure.

TAKE THE MOMENT. YOU DESERVE THE TIME
TO FEEL THE PAIN,
THE ANGER, THE LOSS, AND THE HURT.
ALLOW YOURSELF TO CRY, TO LAUGH,
TO BE SILENT AS IT IS YOUR MOMENT.
YOU CAN'T HELP OTHERS
WITHOUT TAKING CARE OF YOURSELF.
TAKE THE MOMENT.

You have to let go, to reflect, regret, and learn to work through it. The loneliness is welcome at times. At other times, you may want to rail at your demons of injustice. Learning to challenge your grief or to reach out for help is an essential aspect of healing.

My nights were the worst but also the best as I relived my memories without others watching or trying to make me better. I cried at my loss and processed the real magnitude of my loss during the hours of those long, lonely nights.

I had certain people to call when it was overwhelming. When they answered the phone, I would say, "Talk to me, keep me from going down the rabbit hole." They would talk about anything to bring me back from my despair; laughter always helped. It was and still is helpful to make that call to prevent the overwhelming despair from settling into what I call "going down the rabbit hole." You don't feel so alone. Others share that they miss your loved one, as well.

Roadmap to Self Help and Discovery Key Takeaways:
- ❖ Recognize depression is normal and embrace it with the help of professionals, family, and friends to avoid the dark rabbit hole of despair.
- ❖ Determine who your friends are that would help you with your moments of despair.
- ❖ Take the moments to reflect on your loved one, use them to remember and celebrate them.

Express your emotions:
Did you recognize the need to work through your depression? What were or are your coping mechanisms? Do you understand the necessity of taking your moments? Who do you call when the loss is overwhelming? Make your list and keep it available.

_____

_____

_____

_____

_____

What is your action plan?

_____

_____

_____

5) THE UPWARD TURN

As the days go by, we must learn to adjust as our loved ones are not going to return. We deserve happiness and must learn how to live without them, honoring their lives, and our own.

> As you start to adjust your life without your dear one, your life becomes a little calmer and more organized. Your physical symptoms lessen, and your 'depression' begins to lift slightly. [8]

My upward turn involved speaking about Susie any time I could. I mention her often even to passersby, store clerks, clients, associates—even strangers. I feel that if I speak her name, Susie is always present, and people won't forget her.

At the request of my therapist KT to do something for myself, I contacted girlfriends I had lost frequent contact with (while caring for Susie while she was sick and in and out of the hospital) to set up standing monthly dinner dates. My girlfriends allowed me to talk freely and cry about my loss without making them uncomfortable. Soon, the dinner dates became less about my strife and more balanced about all our lives, and some normalcy returned. In truth, they needed me as much as I needed them. Soon, these social encounters helped me see we all have life challenges. They also felt relieved that they could constructively provide some comfort. A profound thank you to my friends!

I had long lunches and dinners with family, just talking, crying, and supporting one another. One such lunch with my mom, Susie's gramma, led to a productive session of remembering, tackling the what-ifs, and then recognizing the good in others. As the entire waitstaff noticed our strife as I tried to cry into my napkin at times quietly, the waiter arrived with wine and a tray of chocolates stating that, "life can be challenging but whatever the problem, chocolates and wine cures all." They also picked up our tab. PF Chang's earned a couple of customers for life.

Those lunches and dinners away enabled us to escape the somberness of home, to have some alone time, and to return to the living. It helped not only me but also those that attended those lunches and dinners with me.

Instead of wallowing at home, family members and I took our grief with us. Life goes on, and staying cooped up in the house did not heal our hearts. So, we go out, and are not embarrassed at sharing "our moments," whether in laughter, tears, or quiet discussion. These discussions aided me in making the decision to share my journey. Thus, my book was born over many a meal and discussion.

LET'S DO LUNCH.

Roadmap to Self Help and Discovery Key Takeaways:

- ❖ The upward turn is hard, to let go of the grief, make lunch dates, and share your feelings.
- ❖ Schedule dates, let others know you need them, those dates will turn into mutual sharing.
- ❖ Give yourself a break, get out of the house, do something even if it is an effort; heal.

Express your emotions:

What can you do to make that upward turn? Who are your confidantes? Schedule dates with them. Make an action plan, schedule dates, walk, exercise, doctor appointments, keep busy, heal.

_____

_____

_____

_____

_____

_____

_____

What is your action plan?

_____

_____

_____

6) RECONSTRUCTION AND WORKING THROUGH

Learning to move forward without your loved ones is inevitable for healthy grieving. We need to come to terms with their loss. It can feel traitorous, letting go of the grip their loss has on our emotions and ability to return to life, our new normal.

> As you become more functional, your mind starts working again, and you will find yourself seeking realistic solutions to problems posed by life without your loved one. You will start to work on practical and financial problems and reconstructing yourself and your life without him or her. [9]

Our grief protects us from being overwhelmed with all the change occurring in our lives and those around us. The fog of grief envelopes the mind making it easier to digest all the loss and change. Although it can be frustrating, it really is for our own protection as the mind numbs areas that are too hard to process on overload.

> Grief causes a fog to roll into our lives. The fog of grief can affect our ability to think or concentrate. This fog often sets in right after a loved one died. But even after the shock wears off, the fog can linger or come and go for a long time. What happens is that our grief gets so heavy that it surrounds us, clouds our minds, and interferes with our ability to think clearly. We're on overload. [10]

GRIEF CAN AFFECT YOUR THINKING—FOG BRAINS.

The fog of grief starts to lift when you can see past the overwhelming loss and hurt and channel your emotions and actions. Some days it might be getting up and getting dressed, going out of the house, picking up the phone and talking to someone, or cooking a meal. Other days it might be reading a book, doing a puzzle, playing cards, or getting back to some semblance of normalcy. The more you do, the easier it becomes. Give yourself a break when you have foggy mental capacity; it is your body's way of protecting you. Its normal, it's OK. I say, "I have fog for brains," and move on. My belief is that others will cut you slack; if they don't, move on and don't let them make you question yourself.

My 91-year-old mother Shirley broke her hip and moved in with us permanently two months following Susie's death. Going to lunch, the movies, and the zoo enables us to remove ourselves from the home and puts us back with people and everyday life scenarios. Shirley has lost so many in her lifetime, but never a child or grandchild. Her emotional, physical, and financial situation has rocked her to the core. I spend much of my time with her, very thankful for our time together. As I write, we are going on a cruise in a week to leave town, change our surroundings and be thankful for having each other, our time together, and the strong bond of love with our family members. The anticipation gives her something to look forward to and will create new and good memories. Hard to fathom, but life goes on.

I have my own consulting business and teach online at several universities. I focused on my work but realized the fog makes me rethink my words, my thoughts, and my approach. I am kinder to myself and others, recognizing we all have moments of strength and weaknesses. My priorities shifted. What was so important before can be deemed trivial now. Spending time with family is priceless. My clientele is selective as time and flexibility are essential.

Our time together was priceless. Although Susie's physical presence is no longer here, she shall forever live on in our hearts, our minds, and walk with us on our journey until we meet again. Thus, I will say her name often reflecting on her life's journey and allowing me to acknowledge her presence and importance in my life.

> THE LOVE OF FAMILY IS ONE OF LIFE'S GREATEST BLESSINGS.

Remembering Susie, I started writing notes to myself. In the process, I started the concept of writing this book, of creating a children's line of books narrated by Susie, and forming a non-profit to honor her life and her good deeds and to channel her loss within the family in a healing and beneficial way (Susie Q's Kids, Inc.). My time became full of purpose as I realized I was not the same person that I previously was.

I am very selective about who I share my time with and what is important to me: time with my mom and parents, my kids, my grandkids, my family, and my friends, and helping those in need.

Look into your life at what you might have placed on a back burner, at what you thought might be fun or worthwhile but were too busy to focus on before. Look at the things that take up your time—are they really essential? Where you want to spend your time? Does it make a difference?

> FAMILY IS WHERE LIFE BEGINS AND LOVE NEVER ENDS.

Take stock of yourself and what you want to achieve for yourself and for or with others. Be stingy with your time and make that distinction and difference.

Roadmap to Self Help and Discovery Key Takeaways:
- ❖ Don't get frustrated as the fog persists, the haze will lift as your new normalcy occurs.
- ❖ Be selective of who you share your time with, who is good for you, and those that are not.
- ❖ Make a point to push yourself even when you don't want to get dressed, leave the house, talk on the phone as once you start to interact, it becomes easier. Be selective of those you share your time with and remain positive.

Express your emotions:
Do you recognize the fog of loss and coping? Have your priorities changed? What do you want to achieve? Spend your time on something productive, a walk or journaling. Be stingy, you deserve it.

_____

_____

_____

What is your action plan?

_____

_____

_____

7) ACCEPTANCE AND HOPE

Acceptance and hope seem unfathomable but are a part of the grieving process and recovery from the traumatic loss of your loved ones. Life continues, and we need to find a way to honor their lives, live our own lives, and move forward, embracing their love on our journey.

> During this, the last of the seven stages in this grief model, you learn to accept and deal with the reality of your situation. Acceptance does not necessarily mean instant happiness. Given the pain and turmoil you have experienced, you can never return to the carefree, untroubled you that existed before this tragedy. But you will find a way forward. You will start to look forward and actually plan things for the future. Eventually, you will be able to think about your loved one without pain, sadness, yes, but the heart wrenching pain will be gone. You will once again anticipate some good times to come, and yes, even find joy again in the experience of living. [11]

My daughter Susie's first heavenly birthday was within two months of her death. We had a Celebration of Life party focused on her and it connected with an overwhelming sense of loss and sadness. For Susie's second heavenly birthday 14 months after her death, we had her birthday Celebration of Life and the presents focused on the living.

We gathered to celebrate Susie and made 50 duffel bags for children taken from their homes and placed in foster care. These comfort bags called "Q Bags" are named after Susie Q and are intended to provide them with hope, inspiration, solace, essentials, comfort, and pleasure. We filled them with the hygiene and dental needs as well as socks; activity items like coloring books, sticker books, storybooks, crayons, markers, pencils, chalk, bubbles, and puzzles; comfort items like stuffed animals, dolls, and comfort foods; pleasure items like toys, balls, cars, a personal journal, and an inspirational book of quotes to offer inspiration, motivation, support, and love. We wanted to let them know that someone cares.

The love of coming together to celebrate, to aid others, and to do good permeated the air, confirming my resolve to form a non-profit organization to keep Susie's love of life and support of others alive and well. I hope that the children who benefit from those bags know they are loved and that there is an angel in their corner. My girl has to be so proud of her family and friends who remember her fondly and continue to do her bidding by helping others.

To learn more about our non-profit and how you can help, please visit Susie Q's Kids, Inc., at susieqskids.org. Take the opportunity to aid others and honor your loved one with your commitment within the community. For more information, contact me at drmary@susieqskids.org (See Appendix D).

Roadmap to Self Help and Discovery Key Takeaways:

❖ Hope is good; always remember the past but live as they would want you to.

❖ Laughter is good medicine. Place yourself in situations or with people to heal and learn to live again as your new normal, always aware and reminiscent of the past you hold dear.

❖ Get a calendar and make plans, be nice to yourself if you need to change best laid plans.

Express your emotions:

How can you accept the new you and the loss of your loved one? What brings you hope? How can you make a difference? In what situations can you safely learn to laugh and enjoy the companionship of family and friends? Be selfish, cancel plans if you need to, but reschedule.

_____

_____

_____

What is your action plan?

_____

_____

_____

FIVE

UNDERSTANDING AND DEALING WITH GRIEF

DEALING WITH GRIEF

Grief is different for everyone, there is no right or wrong approach. We cannot control others, we cannot forget our loved ones, but we can recreate our "new normal" and live our best lives always remembering and honoring them.

Long (2015) states,

> Grief and loss are complex, multifaceted, and multilayered. Loss and our experience of grief are integrated into our lives, not things we get rid of," and she further stated the following four beliefs: (1) "You are not responsible for how others feel about your grief, (2) Moving on doesn't mean forgetting, (3) Moving on doesn't mean the end of grief either, and (4) Ultimately, you get to define 'moving on' for yourself. [12]

WE MUST EMBRACE PAIN AND
BURN IT AS FUEL FOR OUR JOURNEY. [13]

YOUR GRIEF AND YOUR RESPONSIBILITY FOR HOW OTHERS FEEL – OUR LOVED ONES ARE ONE OF A KIND

Talk about your loved ones often. They are one of a kind. We must learn to let them go from our physical presence and embrace their life, what they valued, and how they touched us. By looking at memorabilia, pictures, and scrapbooks that we have from sharing their lives with us or others, we can revisit our memories. As painful as it may be, it is part of the healing process. Give yourself a break; there is no timeline to touching any of their things, or to looking at pictures, moving their clothes, personal items, toys, books, music, and so forth. Everything comes with time.

My mother moved into Susie's room shortly after Susie passed. Her things were put in boxes for storage in the basement. They have remained sealed. The Christmas decorations remain boxed away and new traditions were born. Do things in your own time. It's OK.

These memories are a measure of healing. When we are hit with a memory from a visual connection, a smell, a sound, a place, a person, in so many different ways, it can take us to our knees, to a heart-wrenching crying storm or to a moment of anger. During these times we must let our emotions erupt and then pull ourselves up and remember that they loved us, and we loved them. They would not want us to wallow in our grief and not move forward. So, find something of interest to invest your time into to heal. Talk to others, volunteer—whatever works.

AN AVID DETROIT LIONS FAN

We are avid Detroit Lions football fans with season tickets. Susie only attended one game during her last year. The other days she was in the hospital. Our game time was valuable: together, we would watch, yell, and cheer our team for the away games in the hospital to the laughter of the nursing staff who peeked in whenever we got really excited and loud. But home games, she would insist we go (mom, dad, and grandpa) and we took a guest with her ticket. Susie dressed in her Lions regalia and watched the game, sending a picture to us and us to her, and then the trash-talking commenced via text throughout the game.

As the Lions season began this year, my Facebook memory showed Susie in numerous photos smiling in her regalia, prepped for the game. The fact that each photo was taken in a hospital room broke me with a long, hard heart-wrenching cry. The reality was that Susie still enjoyed life. She still laughed, cried, shared her dreams, cheered her team, and lived to the best of her ability—better than some of us who take life for granted. So, I proudly wear a jersey honoring her with Number 1 on the front and Susie Q on the back. We rub her name for good luck for the Lions, which does not always work.

We sing karaoke at the stadium, singing what we sang at her deathbed: "You are My Sunshine." She may not be there physically, but she is as she was in life, with us always. An excellent job on the field will get a pat on my back on her name because she is watching right along with us. I feel so close to her there remembering the laughter (or frustration) of their plays.

I wrap myself in a blanket her sister Angela made for me from all of Susie's Lions wear (priceless): shirts, hoodies, jerseys, and crying towels, so she is always close. I really can hear and feel her with us, a true fan hanging out with her crazy family.

Angela had a sign placed on the Lions Ford Field scoreboard during the last game of the season with a picture of Susie and me smiling during the only game she attended that year and another sign honored mom, dad, and grandpa:

IN LOVING MEMORY OF THE BIGGEST LIONS FAN
AND RAY OF SUNSHINE."
– SUSIE MCBRIDE-WELSH
8/7/85 - 6/1/17

"HAPPY NEW YEAR MARY,
JOE AND BASIL WELSH. GO, LIONS." ANGELA MCBRIDE

So special. Look for the new memories you create, remembering them, and the way others react to their loss and your feelings and emotions.

You are not the only one impacted by their loss. Understand, death makes everyone uncomfortable. Those experiencing the loss are adjusting just like you. Those who are or are not as significantly impacted, such as friends, work associates, or others you come in contact with may find death uncomfortable; they don't know how you feel, they are afraid of saying the wrong thing or bringing up the subject and making you sad. Your approach and response to them can trump their fear of discussing your loved one, of addressing you, or being with you.

Raising your awareness and approach to them can make communication easier. Try to be aware of their feelings, reluctance, actions, or words that you might find offensive like, "It's time to move on." They mean well but have just not experienced the depth of your loss. They truly cannot comprehend it. Before your loss, did you understand the debilitating affect it had on others who had lost children? I didn't and still can't. Everyone is different.

Learn to forgive them for actual or perceived faults, words or actions; it is therapeutic for you to let the disappointment, anger, or frustration go. It may take time; educate them by sharing your feelings in the moment, as it may also help them. They may not really understand how their words, actions, or inaction hurt you.

People mean well. Some will talk, others will internalize and ignore the topic. Others want to fix you ("Pull yourself together." "Stop crying." "Move on."). Your relationships will change. You will create new relationships with those who share the same or a similar situation.

You might end relationships that remain unhealthy and encourage your healthy relationships to talk and understand you. And you need to forgive yourself and come to terms with the situation.

> IT ALL STARTS WITH YOU!
> YOU ARE IN CONTROL.
> DO WHAT IS RIGHT
> FOR YOU.

It can be hard to recover from the emotional abyss, which can be all-consuming and hard to recover from. Recognize the signs. Let the person or persons you contact help you. Many times in a discussion, a heart-wrenching cry and plea for help can end with resignation as you talk through it or remember something with laughter which is a welcome reprieve to the despair you are facing.

I have reached out to people with those heart-wrenching cries that say, "just talk to me." Sometimes, I just started dialing to get the lucky person who answers the phone: my husband, my sisters, my brother, and friends.

Once, my brother Jim answered and started asking me about doctors, medicines, and so forth. When I said, "just talk," he understood and eventually, the funny memories were brought up and I started laughing at the antics of the past. The call ended with "thanks," letting him know that if I didn't challenge the overwhelming feelings of the moment, I would have gone down the rabbit hole of depression—not a good place.

My sisters Carol, Sandy, Pam, Linda, and Barb got the calls and showed up shortly thereafter with hugs, and then the grief became bearable.

Reach out. You don't have to go through it alone—it is not a sign of weakness! Others want to help but don't know how. Your reaching out allows them to engage and mourn as well.

A grieving mom lamented online about her overwhelming situation and ranted about how to move forward. I replied with some understanding and with ideas to celebrate her son, empathized with her housing arrangements, and shared mine. The conversation ended with mutual support, consideration, a chuckle moment, and thanks. Sometimes, we just need to talk, to get it out. It doesn't change our loss, but maybe it makes it a little easier to bear. Be open and receptive.

Roadmap to Self Help and Discovery Key Takeaways:
- ❖ Nurture healthy relationships and let others go; you are in control.
- ❖ You can't control others, but you can control how you respond and who you connect with.
- ❖ Make sure your support team understands·your immediate needs by a buzzword. Mine was "keep me from going down the rabbit hole, just talk."

Express your emotions:
Who would you contact? Discuss it with them so they know what you expect if they get the call. What are your plans to cope? How does addressing it help you focus your grief and gain some measure of peace? Remember others may be insensitive in their words, your actions are yours, so do what is best for you! Be responsible for healthy relationships and end unhealthy ones.

_____

_____

_____

What is your action plan?

_____

_____

_____

MOVING ON DOESN'T MEAN FORGETTING

Continue to talk, believe, dream, inspire, and be thankful for the time you shared and the memories you created. Look back upon those memories. It is extremely important to keep your loved one alive in your heart by telling their stories, for they are truly never gone if you continue to speak about them on your journey of loss and recovery.

> "IN THE FACE OF EVENTS THAT THREATEN TO OVERWHELM OUR LIVES, STORYTELLING GIVES US A WAY OF RECLAIMING OURSELVES AND REAFFIRMING OUR CONNECTIONS WITH OTHER PEOPLE—THOSE WHO LISTEN TO OUR STORIES AND, BY DOING SO, BEAR WITNESS WITH US."
> (VICTORIA ALEXANDER, N.D.).[14]

Share your life of kindness and caring with others and give of yourself. Look for the beauty that surrounds you, make sure that you value the people in your life. Even

BRAVERY COMES FROM OWNING OUR STORY, THE LOSS OF OUR LOVED ONES, AND OURSELVES.

when you are hurting, it is important to value the relationships you have with others. I learned on my journey that my family and friends are also experiencing loss and/or have disappointments, losses, and challenges they are dealing with. We all need to talk, share, and support each other. That is the true value of friendship—how we react also impacts them.

My house and life are full. Following Susie's death, my 90-year-old mother, Shirley, moved in permanently following hip surgery. Two adult

LIFE IS TO NOT TO BE TRAVELED ALONE. YOU DO NOT HAVE TO JOURNEY IT ALONE.

daughters also moved home, and we watch our 4-year-old grandson Luke two days a week. My husband's parents, Judy and Basil, moved in temporarily for seven weeks following back surgery. The house had never been so full.

One day while cleaning, I swept the hall, got to the end, and found a penny from heaven. Somehow, I tripped or lost my balance and bumped the wall. my mind was elsewhere. I knocked a ceramic bust of Susie off the wall and she shattered—it just broke me. I screamed, threw the broom, and left the house sobbing. Two blocks later, I decided to return home. The tears had subsided and my composure improved.

The hall was swept, the bust of Susie placed gently on the counter broken, chipped, and marred. I felt bad upon my return as my mom cried and said she needed me to hold her, she needed me.

I hugged her but said, "Sorry, mom, I can't fix you. My life is shattered beyond control. I'm sorry." I walked away and left her alone. I did not want to fix anyone. My husband cancelled dinner plans, and we held each other, cried, and slept. Everyone left us alone. When we awoke, we talked about things. I just needed my moment to mourn.

Susie's sister Angela came over and said she would fix the bust and keep her. I didn't need to see Susie "broken," but Angela wanted her anyway, as we got the statue on a trip together—it was only fitting. Susie's brother Jim said, "We just need to go on another trip to get another copy made"— such a simple response. He believed Susie was telling us to take a trip and escape. In other words, to continue living.

It is all about perspective. Try to remain positive and look for the bright side of the situation, if possible.

Knowing how you respond to others affects you and affects your story of how you handle the loss of your loved one. The connection can be inspirational, can motivate others, and can commit them to make changes, it can aid in their recovery and prevent mental health issues. Sharing your story or beliefs, listening to other's words, actions, or inability to act, may help someone avoid suicidal thoughts. It is such an important topic and should be encouraged, not avoided.

SHARE YOUR STORY.

We are all responsible for the mental health of our family, friends, associates, and ourselves. Suicide awareness is critical to the prevention of suicides which happen when a person cannot see a way past the fog of their disappointment, pain, loss, or other overwhelming condition that is affecting their rational thought process. A kind word, thought, or gesture just might save the life of someone in need. Stay connected and aware, acknowledge the efforts of others, empathize with their losses and their conquests, and how they deal with grief.

"THE MOST IMPORTANT THINGS IN LIFE ARE CONNECTIONS YOU MAKE WITH OTHERS." (TOM FORD, N.D.).[15]

WE ARE NOT MEANT TO BE ALONE. REACH OUT AND CONNECT WITH OTHERS.

Roadmap to Self Help and Discovery Key Takeaways:

❖ We all need to talk, share, and support each other. That is the real value of friendship--how we react also impacts them. We are not meant to be alone, reach out to others.

❖ Moving on does not mean forgetting, it is healing and what your loved one would want.

❖ Suicide is not the answer, reach out for help if you have thoughts of self-harm. You are needed, your loss would be felt by many others and not change the present situation.

Express your emotions:

What was or is your breaking point? How do you handle it and ask for assistance/count on others? Have you discussed suicide with your family and friends in general? For yourself or to aid them? Consider that your discussion could prevent an avoidable situation.

_____

_____

_____

What is your action plan?

_____

_____

SUICIDE AFFECTS US ALL – OUT OF THE DARKNESS

Susie and our family strongly support the American Foundation for Suicide Prevention (AFSP) and Tragedy Assistance Program for Survivors of military loss (TAPS). We have been strongly affected by the loss of friends and family members, who have been unable to cope with their challenges, and a family friend, Specialist Keith William Beaupre, who suffered from Post-Traumatic Stress Disorder (PTSD). Although they sought professional help and were surrounded by close-knit family, they took their own lives. Our family will never be the same. We miss them terribly and wonder what more we could have done to help them through their issues.

In Loving Memory of Specialist Keith William Beaupre

SUICIDE TAKES THE LIVES OF TOO MANY AND ALTERS THE
LIVES OF THEIR LOVED ONES.
WE WALK FOR AFSP AND ENCOURAGE PEOPLE TO BE OPEN
AND HONEST ABOUT THEIR CONCERNS.
SUICIDE IS UNSPEAKABLE, AND TO SPEAK IT IS SOMEHOW
TO BRING IT INTO A
HUMAN, IMAGINABLE SPHERE, EVEN IF ONLY IN THE
MOMENT OF SPEAKING.
THE NEED TO TELL IS BOTH A NEED TO TELL ONESELF AND
A NEED TO BE HEARD.
TELLING AND BEING HEARD ARE THE FIRST STEPS
TOWARD RECONNECTION.

VICTORIA ALEXANDER, (1991).[16]
"IN THE WAKE OF SUICIDE: STORIES OF THE
PEOPLE LEFT BEHIND"

When a friend mentions mental illness or suicide or is unable to move past their situation, make sure to reach out. If you see a Facebook post that seems off, connect. If they state something that seems out of sorts, stop and address it. Just taking the time to inquire can potentially talk someone off the ledge, preventing them from thinking others would be better off without them, that life is not worth living, and/ or that there is no hope—let them see the light at the end of the tunnel. Let them know that they matter and make a difference to you—and they have a friend.

My friend Karen needed someone to listen, to know someone other than family heard her. I told her she mattered, and that she needed to walk with us at the next AFSP Out of the Darkness event for herself and to raise awareness for others. She matters! Let others know they do matter, even if they are unable to see it. Help them see it!

Consider investing time in discussing suicide awareness with your family members. It may just allow you to prevent them for thinking in despair that suicide is their only option. Additionally, it may open the conversation for them to have an impact on the lives of someone they know or meet. It brings suicide out of the closet and takes it from a taboo subject to one that should be a topic of conversation. We are responsible to be aware of others and what they are battling. Are they suffering from PTSD? Are they being bullied? Are they ending a relationship? Enduring postpartum depression? Are they suffering from a real or a perceived loss?

Pick up the phone, send a text, a Facebook message, an email, or physically visit them. Encourage them to talk to a therapist, visit their doctor, or go to urgent care or the hospital to address their anxiety or depression. Go with them if you are concerned. Take them to get help. We can all make a difference if we show we care! Be there! You can be the difference!

Our daughter, Dusty, had a meltdown one evening from stress-related issues. Although she doesn't believe in therapy and medicine, she agreed to go to urgent care. The doctor took time to speak with Dusty, who took anxiety medicine temporarily and was able to put things in perspective. She just needed the extra assistance of someone objective speaking to her about her issues and feelings and helping her get a grip on the situation. It changed Dusty's beliefs about therapy and the use of limited medication. Your listening and providing help could be the difference. Show that you care.

I have reached out to let others know that they matter (you know who you are), supported their causes, helped them by getting them out of the house, showing them the beauty of the zoo, the gardens, enjoying a long lunch and talking, and being their advocate when they can't speak for themselves. That simple form of communication might be just what they need to know they are not alone: they matter.

To my friends and family, I am always here with unconditional love. If I don't have the answer, I will try my best to help you get the help you need and will always be there emotionally.

What can you do to make a difference and never regret saying, "If I only knew?" Be aware and care! Being you might just save a life that you were unaware of was in danger or put someone on the road to good mental health.

> REMEMBER, EVERYONE HAS A STORY OR HAS LOVED OR LOST SOMETHING.

If you are in crisis, call The National Suicide Prevention Lifeline at 1-800-273-TALK (8255). American Foundation for Suicide Awareness (AFSP) does not provide its own crisis hotline service (See Appendix D).

My friend Denise and her husband lost their son to suicide. They focused their healing on helping others understand they matter by making beautiful garden art. They donate all their proceeds from Chasing Butterflies to Michigan suicide prevention organizations. Thanks, Denise.

This year, our nonprofit, Susie Q's Kids, supported the Out of the Darkness event by operating the kid's area, brightening and inspiring children, and greeting those impacted by suicide offering an encouraging word or hug. Family and friends honored our loved ones and gave back in the community hopefully changing the view of suicide and offering hope to others,

Roadmap to Self Help and Discovery Key Takeaways:

- ❖ Mental health is real; seek outside help to discover ways to cope with your loss.
- ❖ Recognize we all have personal battles, reach out to others to get help or offer help as it may just prevent a suicide situation.
- ❖ Keep your mental health positive, journal, seek professional help, learn depression triggers, and create a game plan to work through them.

Express your emotions:

Have you or someone you know had suicidal thoughts? Have they been so despondent that you were afraid for yourself or them? What would you do? How can you raise your awareness of others and share your own insecurities?

_____

_____

_____

_____

What is your action plan?

_____

_____

_____

MOVING ON DOESN'T MEAN THE END OF GRIEF, EITHER

The painful realization that our loved ones are gone can either be what allows us to heal or do us in. Those who can channel their grief into something positive can travel the path of life. We have all met people who live in the past. They fail to overcome their challenges, real or perceived. They are never truly happy, living in a world of anger, regret, and hurt. Others pick up the pieces and begin to move forward in what I refer to as their "new normal."

When it comes to grief for a loved one, gone is that person who lived prior to their loved one's loss. The new person has been impacted by the loss in that their priorities in life are different. Their time commitments have changed. Perhaps their willingness to volunteer may increase. The loss has an impact on their commitment to self-discovery, improvement, and health.

Healing involves making changes that channel your grief positively. These include talking with others, seeking professional help, volunteering, and organizing new initiatives. Others may negatively deal with their loss by turning to anger, withdrawing from life and relationships. They may turn to alcohol and drugs and tend to end up ruining their relationships by ending them in divorce, separation, or by simply withdrawing.

Personally, it all takes time. Each day is a struggle. Some days getting out of bed is a chore, taking care of personal hygiene non-important, and withdrawing from others easy. I didn't want to deal with others. I wanted to wallow in my own sorrow, loss, and grief. Other days, it made me reflect on what an impact Susie Q had during her life, what was important to her, how I could honor her contributions to us by enriching our lives, and how my sadness was affecting others around me.

Visiting my daughter Angela one afternoon as she was moving, I stood in the Susie Q area of her loft and the tears started to flow. When she saw me, she said, "No, stop crying—not in the Susie corner. This is my healthy spot, my reflection spot, my favorite spot remembering her."

My reply was that they were not sad tears, they were tears of joy as she had memorabilia and pictures entwined with her beautiful plants telling their life story together. Happy smiles, antics, photos, and memorabilia shared their deep sisterly love and adoration for each other. What I took from that encounter was although Susie is physically gone, she holds that space of importance daily in all our lives.

Susie's brother Jim and wife Karly have the same type of shelving of important memorabilia and ashes for his sister Susie and her brother Keith, who hold places of honor in the family. The kids talk freely about them, share stories, and remember them and learn more through our discussions about them, sharing their angel days with balloons or birthday celebrations of life. We will always miss them; however, they are alive with us if we continue to talk about them.

My grandson Luke has lost his special Aunt Susie and Uncle Keith. One day when we drove past the Tank Arsenal, he saw the army tanks, and he told me, "Uncle Keith drove the tanks." I replied, "Now as an angel, he helps the soldiers to keep them safe."

It made him happy. Now when we pass the Tank Arsenal, Luke says, "Uncle Keith helps the soldiers who drive the tanks, he is an angel." The stories keep our loved ones alive and provide us with comfort.

I fondly remember being at the funeral home standing next to Susie when the three-year old grandkids (Luke and Ella) came running up to the casket and rubbed Susie's arm, saying, "We love you Susie." Life was right in the moment. I knew their love would not diminish; we would keep it strong. Today, a floating dandelion puff gets a "we love you, Susie." A cloud formation might bring up "are Susie and Keith floating on the cloud?" or as we pass the Tank Arsenal, "Uncle Keith drove a tank, now he is an angel watching over the other soldiers driving the tank."

Their legacies are alive. Our pictures have big smiles and 'thumbs up' in honor of our crazy, fun-loving girl Susie and Keith.

The "Thumbs-Up Revolution," raise a thumb for a loved one. When you reflect on the picture, they will be represented in that thumbs-up gesture. Always and forever with you. Share your photos. https://www.facebook.com/ Thumbs-Up-Revolution-1073516522838068/

Roadmap to Self Help and Discovery Key Takeaways:

- ❖ Moving on is not forgetting; it is creating your new you and adjusting.
- ❖ Create new ways to honor your loved one, like thumbs up in a picture.
- ❖ Healing involves making changes that channel your grief positively.

Express your emotions:

How are you moving on? How are your adjusting to your new situation and "new you"? How can you positively channel your thought to aid in your healing process? What special story or activity do you share? Who would you raise a thumb for? Join the Thumbs-Up Revolution.

_____

_____

_____

_____

_____

What is your action plan?

_____

_____

_____

ULTIMATELY, YOU GET TO DEFINE "MOVING ON"

In my opinion, there is no getting over grief. There is only moving on. Some days it is two steps forward and three backward. Other days it is a sprint without looking back. How we process moving on is how we look at life. Are we optimistic, positive people? Then perhaps that will allow us to find that "new normal" more quickly, but always mourning their loss and perhaps our "old normal." If we are not an optimistic person, the challenge may be harder, but it must occur, as our loved ones would never want us to live a life of despair and agony.

Find something to bring you some measure of peace. I talk about Susie all the time to total strangers. Some patiently listen while others try to move away from the discussion. Use your judgement on what works, there is no script for the right way to grieve. Don't

KEEP MOVING FORWARD.

be afraid to seek assistance, whether it is with family and friends, professional help, spiritual guidance, or some other route.

Roadmap to Self Help and Discovery Key Takeaways:
- ❖ There is no getting over grief. There is only moving on.
- ❖ Our loved ones would never want us to live a life of despair and agony.
- ❖ Find your moments of peace and relish them.

Express your emotions:
What are you doing to prepare to move on? Are you positive or negative? How does that impact your ability to move on? Celebrate your moments of peace, write them down for reflection.

_____

_____

_____

_____

_____

_____

_____

What is your action plan?

_____

_____

_____

SIX
GETTING HELP

I t is essential to understand that professional help and support groups can help you deal with your grief. Getting help is not a sign of being incompetent or pathetic. It is a sign of strength. Being able to speak about your feelings enables you to deal with the thoughts you have, to address the depression that follows grief, to obtain medication or sleeping aids to help manage your loss if necessary, and to learn techniques others have used to progress through the grieving process. Understand that you are building your "new normal" as you grieve. The "old you" is forever changed! Your life is different than it was prior to your loved one's death. You must come to terms with your "new normal." Your situation has changed, and you must find a new way to exert your passion and purpose in life. It could be through an aggressive self-care program of diet, exercise, and self-reflection or through volunteering in some capacity to help others, thus continuing your loved one's legacy and providing you with a purpose.

> YOUR NEW CHAPTER:
> ACCEPT THE NEW YOU
> AND YOUR NEW NORMAL.

When this purpose [a sense of meaning or purpose in one's life] is lacking or unclear, a general indifference toward life may be experienced. Difficult times may be far less terrifying or devastating when a lasting meaning to one's life is already present or can be developed through the work of therapy. Without such meaning or purpose, even small challenges can grow and feel overwhelming, confusing, and painful. Therapy can help in regaining touch with lasting values, beliefs, needs, and goals and in treatment, a sense of meaning and purpose can be built around these. Techniques such as meditation, dreamwork, and other powerful tools for getting in touch with inner guidance can also be explored in treatment, and with these techniques, a sense of purpose and meaning that may lend a renewed structure to life can often be regained. [17]

Your mental health awareness is critical to your happiness; seek out professional help. Your therapist can encourage you to speak about your experiences, how your feelings have impacted your grieving journey, and what your future might involve, and how it might evolve.

My journey involved weekly sessions with my therapist KT and eventually changed to bi-weekly meetings. She allows me to discuss all facets of my life and my new normal. My monthly grieving parents' support group allows my husband and I to share common fears, goals, and challenges of learning to cope and live on without our loved one. Our Susie will be forever cherished and woven into our lives past, present, and future.

Roadmap to Self Help and Discovery Key Takeaways:
- ❖ Self-development involves speaking with others.
- ❖ Your new normal involves understanding and processing the impact of the stages of grief.
- ❖ The past, present, and future should positively incorporate your loved one and your love.

Express your emotions:
Have you discussed your situation with your physician and/or a therapist? Are you open to discussing your thoughts with an impartial third party trained to help you? Do you understand how you respond is based on your understanding and coping of the past, present, and future? Share your feelings.

_____

_____

_____

_____

_____

_____

What is your action plan?

_____

_____

_____

PROFESSIONAL HELP

I strongly encourage everyone to seek professional guidance to speak with an impartial third party, to channel your thoughts and feelings in a productive venue, thus enabling you to cry, rant, talk, and focus your goals and objectives on a positive versus negative wavelength. Through talking, you can release some of the what-ifs, if-onlys, the buts, the one-mores, the anger, the thoughts of inadequacy in dealing with the situations leading up to the loss and afterward. It can also help you to focus on which techniques can enable you to move forward toward finding that "new normal," as the loss has changed you and others forever.

My therapist, KT has enabled me to speak freely about whatever is happening in my life. I have taken guests to see my therapist, allowing KT to meet those involved in my life and to encourage my loved ones to also seek guidance. My guests have spoken freely, shared their feelings, addressed my involvement with them or others, and it demonstrated to KT their importance in my life and the support system that I have. The process has allowed others to seek guidance that they might not have as they felt it was a sign of weakness or was not for them. By talking and caring, you aid others in their grieving process. Some never seek professional help as they are afraid or don't believe they need it or that it will help. My approach demonstrated how much it helped me and opened their awareness that it might aid them as well.

BRAVERY COMES FROM KNOWING WHEN TO ASK FOR HELP. HAVE COURAGE TO BE HONEST WITH YOURSELF.

Some days I was barely able to talk through my tears to my therapist, speaking solely about Susie; other days the reality of life and the situations that arose were the main topic of the day. Some days, I talked about things that I didn't plan to speak about, sometimes wondering where the messages originated. It arrived from being comfortable with my therapist and just letting my thoughts take flight, discussing how to get over things from the past, how they impact us, how others influence us, and how to handle current and future situations.

The first year was full of many firsts: first birthday, Mother's Day, Father's Day, first wedding, first birth, and first holidays. Some were just unbearable to plan for. KT let me talk, share my fears, cry, laugh at some of Susie's past antics, and learn how to handle the situation surrounding the upcoming event myself, and with my family and friends.

My main takeaway was that the anticipation was worse than the actual day or event. I had traumatized myself prior with all the "what-ifs," the "just one mores," the guilt, loss, and the anger. By taking a more positive approach on the day, it allowed me to get through it and to also help those around me who many times looked to me for support and guidance.

> THERE IS A PURPOSE FOR PAIN. IT CAN MAKE OR BREAK YOU. EMBRACE IT AND DON'T LET IT BREAK YOU.

I planned different events to celebrate or sometimes just made my regrets to a wedding, shower, or funeral because I did not want my sadness to impede upon the specialness of the day or didn't want to deal with the rawness of loss and despair that my loved one will not attend or experience. Allow yourself to do what is best for you!

Others accepted and honored my decisions. Don't be afraid to speak up for yourself or others; do what is best for you in the moment. Remember, this is your path to discovery and creation of your "new normal." If others do not understand, then it is time to re-evaluate their friendship and perhaps realize what they might be personally dealing with as well.

I attended a wedding and about 25 minutes before the service, I silenced my phone. I glanced at Facebook while waiting and an extraordinary message from my daughter surfaced on Facebook memories telling me how awesome she thought I was and thanking me for always being by her side, loving her and being her best friend. I lost my composure; without any explanation, I left the service and went for a two-block walk crying over the injustice.

A woman stopped and backed her car up to ask if I was all right. When I said yes, she said, "You clearly are not." We talked for a few minutes about the recent loss of her husband and the loss of my daughter and how we both needed to continue life and that it was simply Susie's way to tell me it was OK and that she felt my pain and wanted me to know she was OK. The woman had recently lost her husband and could connect with my pain. I dried my tears and made it in before the service started.

Be aware of those around you: a kind gesture just might help someone and help you as well. The kind lady said she had been thinking of her husband and felt she got a message from him from the encounter and vowed to have a better day herself. How we act and react makes a difference for us but can also impact others, or you can become that role model for others. I hear my words coming from my grandson, Luke: "Oh, my goodness," "you silly goofball," "put your thumbs up" and "smile."

We never truly understand how much we mean to and influence others. Be you, be unique, be kind to yourself, and share your specialness with others as they value your friendship.

STRENGTH COMES FROM ASKING FOR HELP. YOUR JOURNEY SHOULD NOT BE ALONE. BE BRAVE AND ASK FOR HELP.

Roadmap to Self Help and Discovery Key Takeaways:

❖ Seeking help is not a sign of weakness; it takes strength to deal with loss and adjustment.

❖ Be open to sharing because others may need your comfort as much as you do, and it helps to talk.

❖ Don't be afraid to speak up for yourself or others; do what is best for you in the moment.

Express your emotions:

What kind of help and assistance have you requested? Have you shared your insecurities with your loved ones to help you cope? Talk to others and encourage them to seek help. Be kind to yourself. What have you done for yourself, you must take care of you before you can help others?

Who are your close confidants? Have you made a point of scheduling lunch or dinner to make sure those visits happen? Put them on the calendar so you can't put it off or avoid them.

_____

_____

_____

What is your action plan?

_____

_____

_____

GRIEVING GROUP

There is also group therapy, where people in a like-minded situation can find comfort and solace by speaking to others who have or may be experiencing the same or similar feelings. You can ask your therapist or search online for groups located in your area or online to help you. By finding a group, you can talk freely about your situation and listen to them as well; your common circumstances allow for sharing without making others uncomfortable. You might learn from the way they coped, and most of all, know that you are not alone in your situation. You might make new relationships forged on your mutual bond which are beneficial to all.

We found a grieving parent group, The Bereaved Parents of USA, Macomb County Chapter, which meets once monthly, www.bereavedparentsusa.org (See Appendix D).

Please look for a chapter in your area or another similar type of organization for support. Each parent can share something about their child and themselves, and then we have group discussions on topics of interest. Upon the birthday month or angel birthday month (day they left us) of your child, you can present a story or situation about your child (sort of a show and tell scenario) to inform the members about your child. We celebrate with desserts and foods supplied by the parents on their celebration month, a way to say happy birthday to our loved ones, to comfort, laugh, or cry. Our contribution for Susie always includes her favorite candy: Jolly Ranchers and a yellow Funfetti birthday cake.

We are so glad we found this group. It has enabled us to do things outside of the monthly meeting as a group and make individual friendships based on our shared grief, which has evolved into simple friendships and outings together. It warms my heart to think our angel babies may be watching over us and smiling down upon us, happy that we have found solace in each other.

This book was written in the second year of my self-discovery following Susie's death. I find myself gravitating to the new members who are so lost in their grief to welcome them to a group none of us ever wanted to join. I allow them to talk, cry, or listen, always extending my phone number if they wish to talk afterward. Their loss is palpable—you can feel their sadness, anger, loss, and disbelief. Sharing our journey hopefully provides them with some comfort, and listening to them hopefully lets them know they are not alone in the despair of losing their child. I find speaking about Susie is also good therapy for us. At times I am talkative, and at other times, I pass, choked up, and unwilling to speak up, as the loss is too overwhelming and raw.

I strongly encourage you to look for the group that connects with you. There are many different types of groups: for parents, siblings, on-ground or online, for babies lost before they had a chance to experience life or those that were here a short time or a longer time, for loss of a parent, loss of a significant other—loss knows no bounds. If you do not connect with a particular therapist or group, look for another, we are all different and no one situation is ideal for everyone. Just like finding that comfort zone with your family physician, hairdresser, or mechanic, you must find someone you trust to whom you can share the experiences of your loss. Keep trying until you feel you can say anything, and thus allow healing to begin. I give my gratitude to my therapist KT, the Bereaved Parents group, and my family and friends, for allowing me to speak freely and heal. Good luck on your journey!

THERAPY IS GOOD. IT CAN AID YOU WITH YOUR GRIEF JOURNEY. EMBRACE IT.

91

Roadmap to Self Help and Discovery Key Takeaways:

❖ Connect with a group—your common circumstances allow for sharing without making others uncomfortable.

❖ Your close bond may forge relationships with others beyond the scheduled meetings.

❖ Sharing allows you to honor your loved one, give others some intimate insights, and allows you to address the challenges involved in surviving the loss of our loved ones.

Express your emotions:

Have you spoken with your physician? A therapist? A grieving group? Support group? Lunch/dinner dates with friends? Are you aware of others and how you might impact their healing and mental health? Connect, it helps to talk about our loved ones and our feelings.

_____

_____

_____

What is your action plan?

_____

_____

_____

BUTTERFLIES

Butterflies are symbolic. A butterfly caterpillar completely transforms into a chrysalis (or pupa) and when ready, emerges (or e-closes) as a butterfly. I liken this to our situation of death and rebirth as a "new you, your new normal" emerges.

Sometimes you don't realize the weight of something until you feel the weight of its release. [18]

Butterfly Release

Many of our parents from our support group believe in the majesty of the butterfly and its symbolic message. They have dedicated gardens and plants to encourage the birth of butterflies. This year our grieving group had a butterfly release for our children in a special commemorative garden. Each angel was represented by a donated butterfly where we discussed our children briefly and then released them to start their life journey taking us with them, letting us think freely, releasing the pain of our loss, embracing the future when we will reunite, and relishing the present knowing that we need to be present in our lives to honor them, creating our "new normal."

Some events are more comfortable and some harder. It always depends on the moment, the thoughts of the day, the hour, or the minute. I was unable to watch their release thinking of Susie, but was warmed at the thought of them all together released of any pain, free-spirited, floating near us. You must deal with the change that is happening around you; some days are easier than others. Be kind to yourself and others as we travel this path of loss and rebirth.

WHEN WE TALK ABOUT OUR LOSS. THE WEIGHT OF THE
LOSS CAN BE RELEASED.
WHEN WE SHARE OUR LOSS, WE CAN GROW AND
TRANSFORM CREATING OUR NEW NORMAL.

Roadmap to Self Help and Discovery Key Takeaways:
- ❖ The butterfly is symbolic of transformation and rebirth, it resembles those dealing with grief as they transform into their new normal.
- ❖ Embrace the change, always remembering the past and how you can honor them moving forward.

Express your emotions:
Do you think butterflies are symbolic? Do you encourage flowers/ bushes to draw butterflies to your home and garden? Do they make you pause when you see them? Do you find peace in their presence? Look for the beauty around you as you transform.

_____

_____

_____

_____

_____

_____

_____

What is your action plan?

_____

_____

_____

SEVEN
HOW TO DEAL WITH BEREAVEMENT?

Everyone deals with grief differently, learning to deal with bereavement is a personal journey as well as appreciating the journey of friends and family. According to Alan Wolfelt, "bereaved means "to be torn apart" and "to have special needs." Perhaps your most important "special need" right now is to be compassionate with yourself. In fact, the word "compassion" means "with passion". Caring for and about yourself with passion is self-compassion."[19]

Self-care is important as you grieve, you cannot help others when you are not whole yourself. You may never feel whole again, but you can feel love, laughter, and life with a unique awareness of your loved one tucked away in your special place. You can draw on those precious memories to help you one-step-at-a-time; your loved ones would want the best for you.

"Over many years of walking with people in grief, I have discovered that most of us are hard on ourselves when we are in mourning. We judge ourselves and we shame ourselves and we take care of ourselves last. But good self-care is essential to your survival. To practice good self-care doesn't mean you are feeling sorry for yourself, or being self-indulgent; rather, it means you are creating conditions that allow you to integrate the death of someone loved into your heart and soul."[20]

Everyone mourns and moves on differently and giving yourself a break is of utmost importance as you travel your grief journey. Don't constrict yourself with how you should deal with grieving or place time constraints upon yourself. We all deal differently and can be tipped over the edge by a comment, a smell, a sound, an item, a picture, the reality hits home and the sorrowfulness must be released.

Time does lessen the intenseness and frequency, but that underlying trigger can bring it home full force. Take care of yourself in those moments and others on your grief journey. As you learn to deal with your grief and with others, the way you act and react not only has an impact on you but also on those close to you and those with whom you interact. The road of self-help and recovery is not meant to be traveled alone, be kind to yourself and others as it makes the path you travel easier to tolerate.

Remember—self-care fortifies your long and challenging grief journey, a journey which leaves you profoundly affected and deeply changed. To be self-nurturing is to have the courage to pay attention to your needs. Above all, self-nurturing is about self-acceptance. When we recognize that self-care begins with ourselves, we no longer think of those around us as being totally responsible for our well-being. Healthy self-care forces us to mourn in ways that help us heal, and that is nurturing indeed."[21]

Take Care of Yourself

Self-care can be an area where we struggle. Often, we take care of family, friends, work, and home life not placing importance on our own health and well-being. We fail to take the time and commitment to ourselves. Why?

It is essential to reflect on why others, work, or house-work comes first. Take stock of what is important in your life. Make a wellness plan, make an agenda to change your perspective on self-care. You matter.

Make a wellness plan involving exercise, a sound diet, sleep and emotional well-being, embracing life, and your spiritual well-being.

Exercise

Understand the importance of exercise: it makes you feel better; it provides you with more energy, and it gives you a reason to get up and move. Start slow or dive in full force.

Make your plan fit your lifestyle: go to the gym, take a class, work out at home to a video or online program, go for a slow walk, a brisk walk or a run, ride your bike, take up meditation, or yoga. Grab your dog or a neighbor's and walk them. Decide what works best for you and get busy. Once you start exercising, your body will respond with more energy to expend on other avenues of your life. To get up and get moving is the first step!

I have always found it hard to stay on a healthy eating and exercise track. I am starting my diet and hope to increase my level of exercise by walking more steps and

> EXERCISE IS NOT ONLY GOOD FOR THE BODY, BUT ALTERS OUR OUTLOOK, OUR ATTITUDE, AND OUR PERSPECTIVES.

taking a scheduled exercise class. If it is not on the calendar—it usually doesn't happen. Wish me luck!

Roadmap to Self Help and Discovery Key Takeaways:
- ❖ Be compassionate to yourself. Good self-care is essential to your survival.
- ❖ Be selfish: take time for yourself. It will aid your personal development and enable you to help others on their personal journeys.
- ❖ Exercise is not only good for the body, but alters our outlook, attitude, and perspectives.

Express your emotions:
What is your coping mechanism? Perhaps a brisk or leisurely walk? Call a friend and start an exercise program. Take a swim class or yoga class. Start slowly to avoid feelings of failure or despair giving you reason to quit (maybe 2,000 steps—track it on your phone and then increase in increments). Get a buddy and get busy or do it yourself. Just move—get out of the house.

_____

_____

_____

What is your action plan?

_____

_____

_____

Diet

Just as important as exercise is the food we eat. Understanding how your body responds to different foods and drinks will enable you to understand the alignment with your body, mind, and soul. What effect does your dietary plan and consumption of alcoholic and caffeinated beverages have on your physical being? Grief can be debilitating, causing you to over- or under-eat and to eat convenient or comfort foods that might not be the best for your health. It takes effort to eat right, to go shopping for fresh fruits and vegetables, to drink enough water, and to refrain from junk food, caffeine, and alcoholic beverages.

Create a plan starting with meal planning, grocery shopping, establishing meal times, and limiting after hours eating and drinking as this can affect your emotional and physical well-being. Create a plan with family members, friends, and a program like Weight Watchers or medically managed programs. Your success rate will improve, and you may also be doing them a favor. We can all benefit from drinking more water and eating better.

I struggle with this one. I have always struggled with my weight, and the night before my daughter died, I was up late grading papers. She did not feel well, and we had an early morning doctor appointment. She said, "Mom, go to bed. You need to take better care of yourself, or you won't be able to help me or anyone else." She was taken by ambulance to the hospital a couple hours later and never returned home. I have a mental hiccup about my guilt for not taking her earlier and perhaps some self-blaming for not doing so. It takes an effort to eat healthy, to cook, to try to lose weight, to exercise. I was not in a place to do so.

Recognizing my mental capacity, as a family (my husband, another daughter, and I) are starting a medical program to become healthier. Even if we fall off the wagon for a day and splurge, no guilt, let's just start back up again. There is too much to feel guilty about or to doubt ourselves. Give yourself a break. Wish us luck!

A HEALTHY LIFE INVOLVES EXERCISE AND EATING A BALANCED DIET.

Roadmap to Self Help and Discovery Key Takeaways:
- ❖ Aim for proper nourishment and set a plan to get the proper amount of liquids and food into your routine.
- ❖ Accept yourself, don't criticize yourself for your weight: under, on target, or over.
- ❖ Recognize your mental capacity, don't let guilt or frustration wreak havoc on your plan.

Express your emotions:
Do you know your behaviors and triggers that affect your weight gain or loss? What behaviors are working against you, address them. Can you engage yourself and others to try to overcome this challenge? Try, as you will feel better and sleep better with good dietary plans and exercise routines in place. Plan and start your program to better health.

_____

_____

_____

_____

What is your action plan?

_____

_____

_____

Sleep

Sleep can be elusive as the mind has trouble processing your loss, or it can be debilitating as it drains the life from you making it hard to function. Sleep is necessary to refresh your body, your mind, and your heart, trying to grasp its importance in your healing process is critical to your short and long-term health.

According to Joe Leach of Healthline, the following list contains ten reasons why sleep is so important:

1. Poor Sleep Can Make You Fat – sleep duration is associated with a drastically increased risk of weight gain and obesity, in both children and adults.

2. Good Sleepers Tend to Eat Fewer Calories – poor sleep affects hormones that regulate appetite. Those who get adequate sleep tend to eat fewer calories than those who don't.

3. Good Sleep Can Improve Concentration and Productivity – good sleep can maximize problem-solving skills and enhance memory. Poor sleep has been shown to impair brain function.

4. Good Sleep Can Maximize Athletic Performance – longer sleep has been shown to improve many aspects of athletic and physical performance.

5. Poor Sleepers Have a Greater Risk of Heart Disease and Stroke – sleeping less than 7-8 hours per night is linked to an increased risk of heart disease and stroke.

6. Sleep Affects Glucose Metabolism and Type 2 Diabetes Risk – sleep deprivation can cause prediabetes in healthy adults in as little as six days. Many studies show a strong link between short sleep duration and type 2 diabetes.

7. Poor Sleep Is Linked to Depression – poor sleeping patterns are strongly linked to depression, particularly for those with a sleeping disorder.

8. Sleep Improves Your Immune Function – getting at least eight hours of sleep can improve your immune function and help fight the common cold.

9. Poor Sleep Is Linked to Increased Inflammation – sleep affects your body's inflammatory responses. Poor sleep is strongly linked to inflammatory bowel diseases and can increase your risk of disease recurrence.

10. Sleep Affects Emotions and Social Interactions – sleep deprivation may reduce your social skills and ability to recognize people's emotional expressions.

The Bottom Line – along with nutrition and exercise, good sleep is one of the pillars of health.[22]

Not only are exercise, eating, and drinking healthy important, poor sleeping habits and sleep deprivation can also impact your health. As Leach indicated, it can cause concentration and memory issues, productivity to function correctly, increase medical issues, further your depression, reduce your immune system making you more likely to catch colds and battle diseases, as well as coping with others. As you grieve, all these factors play a major part in your ability to cope, to function, to deal with your emotions and those of others, and your capacity to deal with others personally, professionally, and socially.

I spent many hours over my daughter's adult life in and out of hospitals. Our special times were during the evening when others were asleep. We would talk while I graded papers both in the hospital and when she was lucky enough to be home. I still teach and grade papers at night, and my night times are my worst. I never slept well before and still don't. I need to change my habits, as my sleep deprivation plays a factor in my irritability, foggy moments (memory confusion), increased caloric intake, and Diet Pepsi addiction—they go hand-in-hand with my late hours and my health in general.

GRIEF CAN LEAVE YOU PHYSICALLY AND MENTALLY TIRED. TAKE CARE OF YOURSELF.

I also admit that I have an aversion to going to sleep. During my waking hours, I can rationalize and try to understand my loss, but during my sleep, I have a recurring dream that terrifies me. I cry uncontrollably in my sleep, as I am always looking for Susie and cannot find her. The dreams are more pronounced when I have little rest. As a result, I put my body into utter exhaustion mode and avoid sleep, which makes the dream intensity worse. I have received medication for anxiety that I can take to help relax me at night or take over the counter Melatonin to aid in sleeping.

We all cope differently. The point is to talk about it and find ways to address our fears, our anxieties, and our personal demons. Susie visited me in my dreams one day and expressed she was OK and is always with me. The nightmare has stopped. I no longer need to look for her. She assured me she was at peace and with me still. I hope you have the opportunity to experience a visitation from your loved one and find some semblance of peace.

YOUR BODY NEEDS SLEEP TO ADDRESS YOUR PHYSICAL, EMOTIONAL, AND MENTAL NEEDS.

Wish me luck as I try to tackle my eating, exercise, and sleep patterns!

Roadmap to Self Help and Discovery Key Takeaways:
- ❖ Recognize the importance of rest on the mind, attitude, and body.
- ❖ Establish patterns and plans to improve your mental capacity through your sleep patterns.
- ❖ Release guilt and the "what ifs"; embrace the "what I did and how much you cared" outlook.

Express your emotions:
Do your sleeping patterns help or hurt you? Have you talked it over with your therapist and doctor? Have you shared your situations with your loved ones? Get help. You need your sleep.

_____

_____

_____

_____

_____

_____

_____

What is your action plan?

_____

_____

_____

Emotional Well-Being

There is something to be said for taking care of yourself. When you wake more rested, you are more apt to have a positive outlook throughout the day. Set goals for yourself, as your well-being not only sets the stage for your own health and perspective, but also for those you love. We all know those people who have a constant negative outlook on life. It can be so negative and depressing that we try to avoid them. We don't want others to avoid us. We need each other to be able to connect with others, to share our anxieties, our fears, our anger, our apprehensions, our sense of loss, and to share our hopes and dreams. When we place an exerted effort on getting up, making ourselves presentable, and emphasizing speaking and interacting with others, we increase our chances of having a positive day.

WHEN WE ARE POSITIVE. WE CREATE POSITIVE ENERGY.

I try to stay positive in life. I have always approached life with the "cup more full than empty" attitude. My daughter Susie also had this approach. She smiled all the time, even when she was in extreme pain. She wanted to make others feel welcome, happy, loved, and appreciated.

This philosophy helps me get up and put on my game face, even when I don't want to. Perhaps I would rather lie in bed and shut out the world. However, this is not healthy, not what Susie would want, not what is right for me. By getting up, I increase my ability to have a good day, to see others, to interact with others, and to enjoy blessings life has bestowed on me. Each day we enjoy life should be considered a blessing.

SET GOALS FOR YOURSELF.

Every month I schedule my hair appointment. Having

a good hairstyle makes me feel pretty, a big step in conquering the depression surrounding grief. I make appointments with my daughter Angela and my mom to have lunch and get our nails done. It is a scheduled date to get together with her busy schedule and makes us all feel pampered and special, a great feeling.

When Susie was alive, she also enjoyed our date time to get our nails done, it made her feel pretty and was a special time taken out of busy schedules. When she passed, we had her nails painted bright pink, and her sister Angela and I went to get ours done in bright pink as well. Our traditions continue. It is crucial to maintain some and create new ones.

Another way to improve physical health is to ensure you are seeing your doctor for well care, your therapist for psychological care, and treating yourself to a massage occasionally. It keeps the world at bay for a small period of time, reduces the tension and stress in your body, and allows you to recharge—a treat well worth the time and money. You deserve it.

Susie and I had standing monthly appointments for massages. She went more frequently to try to relieve her back and stomach pain and gain some measure of pain relief. It took me ten months to return and start using my massage package after her death. I cried the first time but realized that she is always with me, and it gave me a sense of personal support and continuity of our commitment to a good sense of well-being. Additionally, it helped to release the tensions in my body from the stress of living without her. Treat yourself.

Taking time to place your thoughts on paper or in an online format enables you to see your life differently and to see how it affects your outlook and personal and professional relationships. Journaling is an often-used technique to gather your thoughts: what worked that day for you, what set you off, what inspired you, what made you smile, what accomplishments did you make (regardless of its size), and what motivated you. Once we begin to understand our motivators, we can learn to avoid certain situations and embrace others. We may also learn how our loved ones react to us and make adjustments to improve our communication and interactions with them.

YOUR LEGACY IS BUILT DAILY.

I always have good intentions to journal but find myself lacking in the discipline to do so every day. I want to share things with my daughter Susie and have caught myself picking up the phone, sending a text or email, and then being sad that I cannot; she is no longer with us. She still has a Facebook account; it is memorialized (check out this function for your own knowledge), and I can still send her messages through the Messenger function. I use this option when I want to share something with her, be it my thoughts, my adventures, photos, ideas, poems, quotes, etc. Use your journal or Messenger (or both) to tell your loved ones how you feel, that you miss them, what is going on in your lives, your family and friend's lives, share pictures and memories with them, talk to them as often as you like as if they were still alive. The process to me is comforting; I keep her abreast of current activities and share my thoughts with her as if I would if she was alive.

Roadmap to Self Help and Discovery Key Takeaways:

❖ Embrace each day with a positive outlook, a poem, an activity, anything to change the mental perspective for the day, make it a good one, always remembering your loved one.

❖ Get out of bed, shower, dress, and leave the house, don't dwell on the negative.

❖ You build your legacy daily, make it useful. Make a difference in your own life and others.

Express your emotions:

Take personal care of yourself, your attitude, your outlook, and look for the positive. Share your emotional activities. Who is involved? How does it help? What are your fears and aversions, and how might you tackle them? The first key is to identify them, and then start to address them.

_____

_____

_____

What is your action plan?

_____

_____

_____

Embrace Life

Most likely, life was full before your loved one passed away. The challenge is to keep alive whatever that means to you. Learning how to face your "new normal," understanding you will never be that same person before to your loss, facing your fears, granting forgiveness to yourself and your loved one, offering forgiveness to others for real or suspected infractions, and avoiding suicidal thoughts, are very important.

How do we overcome these feelings and thoughts, embrace a hobby or self-help type of activities? Perhaps looking at old ways of coping and living or trying new types will enable you to heal and move forward. What will make you happier or more content? Try to avoid negative or suicidal thoughts. Your loved ones will survive and move forward if you are no longer in their lives, but they will not be better off without you! Attend any suicide prevention activity and you will see the brokenness of those left behind. They will be forever missing a piece of themselves as a piece of their heart will have gone with you. Assess and prioritize your needs and desires, start to enjoy life and heal.

Some suggestions might be:

❖ Music, listening to music could be soothing or energizing. Or the arts, sing, dance, appreciate the sounds, the melodies, and the memories they may evoke.

    a. Create a library of soothing, energizing, reflective, dancing, or exercising music.

    b. Sing Karaoke and enjoy the company of others.

    c. Take a music class or learn to play an instrument.

    d. Take a dance or exercise class, connecting with the music.

❖ Read and listen to audiobooks. Lose yourself in a good mystery, fiction, thriller, whatever style you like to challenge your brain and keep you learning and enjoying the written word. Visit a library, bookstore, or lose yourself in your Kindle.

   a. Grab a book and lose yourself in the message, whether it's self-help, fiction, sci-fi, or romance.

   b. Can't concentrate or on the go? Consider an audiobook.

   c. Get a puzzle book – Fill-it-in, Sudoku, Crosswords, or Word Search.

   d. Visit your local library, talk to others, and rent a book, audiotape, or movie.

❖ Write and put your thoughts on paper. Write your thoughts, your memories, your desires, your fears, your challenges, your goals and objectives, your stories told or untold, and poems. Bring your words to life.

   a. These words can be shared or kept private.

   b. Your journal can hold your private thoughts, your physical or emotional goals, how you get through the day (perhaps a pattern will evolve to encourage or discourage you).

   c. Your words can put to paper your memories, so they don't diminish over time, to share with others, to allow you to relive and enjoy the memories.

   d. Your goal-writing can help you lose or gain weight, drink more, less, or eliminate a drink, track your exercise goals, steps, and health vitals.

YOUR BELIEFS ARE EXPRESSED IN THE ART OF WRITING.
BELIEVE IN YOURSELF.

❖ Gardening: enjoy the beauty around you. Plant a flower or an herb garden and watch the different seasons blossom. Remember how your loved one cherished a particular flower or fragrance, plant a memorial garden or plant flowers where they are laid to rest.

  a. Get outside, enjoy the sunshine, water the flowers and grass, plants, flowers, or vegetables and watch them bloom.

  b. Enjoy the sights, sounds, smells, the animals that visit: the birds, butterflies, the bees, dragonflies, the bunnies, the squirrels.

  c. Create memorial gardens and watch the flowers, bushes, and trees grow over time.

  d. Add sculptures to your garden: stepping stones, angels, fountains, windchimes.

  e. Add plaques with special sayings or meaning to keep you positive and to remember your loved one.

❖ Go for a walk, run, ride a bike, do something physical. Enjoy the fresh air, breathe in the beauty of nature around you, exercise and energize your body, keep moving by yourself, or interact with others. Take an exercise or yoga class, walk, run, or bike a marathon (set goals).

  a. Get up, get outside, enjoy the solitude of a walk or ride.

  b. Go to the park, talk to others enjoying the outdoors.

  c. Challenge yourself: walk, run, or bike a marathon for a good cause or for the fun of it.

  d. Take an exercise class or join the gym, get out with others that are trying to improve or maintain their physical awareness and socialize.

    e. Take a walk in the neighborhood or a park trail to clear your mind and feel better.

❖ Enjoy a movie, a play, a concert, a sporting event, an afternoon at the museum, the aquarium. Embrace life's pleasures, enjoy the arts, the solitude, or the crowd, lose yourself in the moment.

    a. Getting out of the house is the hardest sometimes. Take in a movie.

    b. Watch the kids or grandkids play sports. Play a sport yourself.

    c. Go to a sporting event, get lost in the couple hours by cheering and supporting your teams.

    d. Visit the art museum, the aquarium, the zoo: enjoy the arts and animals.

    e. Take in an art fair or craft show: buy something new or learn a new trick.

    f. Go to a concert: enjoy the music, sing, dance, and laugh.

❖ Volunteer to help others and use your skills to make someone smile, hold their hand, provide a shoulder to lean on or a hug, make someone feel better, less lonely, appreciated, valued, happy. Make a difference.

    a. What did you enjoy before? What did your loved one enjoy or support?

    b. Find those commonalities and make a difference by volunteering; brighten the day of others, bring them comfort. Share a moment with others.

c. Volunteer to help at a nursing home, a hospital, the zoo, wherever you can make that difference helping enrich the lives of others.

d. Consider starting or partnering with a non-profit to help in a larger capacity.

❖ Enjoy a meal, a favorite or new recipe; experience new and favorite dishes, try cooking at home, or visiting an old or new restaurant. Call an old friend or a new one to share your meal, visit the market to get fresh vegetables, fruits, for your cooking.

a. Make a date, a stand-alone or a weekly or monthly commitment, share a meal together and talk about you, about them, about your loved ones—just talk.

b. Go with your significant other or friend to visit a new restaurant.

c. Go to the local outdoor market, get some exercise, fresh air, and fresh fruit and vegetables to cook with. Better yet, make a date with someone to go with you.

d. Enjoy the prospect of cooking and trying new recipes; share your recipes and meals.

❖ Travel. Relive old memories or create new ones. Go by yourself or with family or friends on a short-day trip (planned or unplanned), a weekend or an extended vacation.

a. Pull out the memory books, the memorabilia, the pictures; relive your trips.

b. Plan a new trip, make new memories; do something you might not have done together.

c. Make it easy, an overnight trip, a weekend getaway, a week or longer adventure.

    d. Go visit family and friends or take on a new experience.

    e. My husband and I have continued to travel. We have gone with our kids and I have taken a cruise with my mom to make her feel appreciated and special.

❖ Focus on yourself, whatever it takes. Visit the hair or nail salon or massage therapist. Spend a few hours at the mall buying something new, take a class, cuddle with a loved one, recharge, and take "me" time and don't feel guilty about it.

    a. You matter. Treat yourself; get a manicure and pedicure, a new hairstyle, schedule massage therapy.

    b. Treat yourself by going to the mall, get something new. "You deserve it."

    c. Take time for yourself. Take that long walk, the time to talk for hours to a long-distance friend, or to have cuddle time with a loved one or favorite animal companion.

    d. Take the time to clean out your closet, your seasonal clothes, your jewelry. Get organized. It's a good feeling. Make it better by donating those rarely used items.

❖ Balance work and family life. Set boundaries, get your rest, drink water to keep hydrated, eat well, give yourself a break, learn to say no, schedule your "me" time so it does not get forgotten.

    a. Saying no may be the hardest thing to do.

    b. When someone is in harm's way, they may need medical or psychological support. You may not be able to walk away, but steer them in the right direction for help.

   c. For others, learn to say no. Be stingy with your time. You deserve to take care of yourself first.

❖ Schedule time for others important in your life: rekindle relationships, form new ones, dedicate time to cherish their time and company.

   a. Schedule dates with current and old friends.

   b. Reach out to rekindle old relationships via phone, email, text message, Facebook, in person.

   c. Look for avenues for making new relationships: the gym, church, support groups, work, and/or with family and friends.

BURNOUT OCCURS WHEN WE FAIL TO ALLOT OURSELVES
ALONE TIME.
BE STINGY AND TAKE THE TIME.

❖ Journal: use journaling to ensure you are finding time for yourself, to reflect on your goals as they change, to value the things important in your life, and to address your own happiness and that of those you love and care for.

   a. Chart your progress.

   b. Track your goals and attainment of them, increase, improve, and add new ones.

JOURNAL YOUR THOUGHTS

❖ Talk about your loved ones often; speak about them any opportunity you can (with the cashier in the store, customer support, neighbors, any appointments, wait staff, work, school, church, whenever).

   a. Never be afraid to speak of your loved ones.

   b. Make it a regular occurrence, it gives others a chance to speak about them as well.

   c. For those uncomfortable with the topic, explain it is important to you that you don't forget them. You understand that talking about them may make you sad or cry, but that is also healing for you. If they are truly uncomfortable, be aware of their feelings and refrain from discussing your loved one or your situation with them.

❖ Find ways to express your love with body art memorializing their impact on you.

   a. Determine the right avenue (temporary or permanent).

   b. Find the best symbolism of your love and how you want to remember and honor your loved one.

   c. Wear it proudly (Ashley and Sam honor Susie with their tattoos).

Roadmap to Self Help and Discovery Key Takeaways:

❖ Assess and prioritize your needs and desires, embrace memories in your new life.

❖ Focus your time of positive activities and refrain from dwelling on the negative.

❖ Talk about your loved one, your situation, your needs, and ask for help and assistance.

Express your emotions:

Search the list, make your list of actions you perform and congratulate yourself. Make a list of others to set as goals and then get busy. The more you talk, the better chance you will have of adjusting to your "new normal," heal and become more satisfied with your new life.

_____

_____

_____

_____

_____

What is your action plan?

_____

_____

_____

Spiritual Well-Being

Regardless of your religious beliefs, there must be a presence of God or a place of peace that invigorates you. Read inspirational quotes or poems to stimulate and motivate you. They may make it easier to deal with life in general and to appreciate your loved ones, yourself, and those around you. In other words, try to stay positive and believe that life is precious. We all have a purpose on this earth. Try to celebrate your loved one's life and hope to reunite in the future.

EMBRACE YOUR PASSION AND PURPOSE.

When a loved one passes, those left behind have choices to grasp the situation. For some, it is denial and they are unable to cope in a healthy manner, turning to drugs and alcohol to try to deal with the depression that descends upon them. Others lose the battle of depression, taking their own lives. Be aware of this in yourself and in your loved ones. Reach out for professional help if needed.

Others turn to one another to address the loss and to cope. When the individual is genuinely a magnet in the family, their passing is a catalyst for change, impacting the mindset of those left behind. As you start to cope, you can energize those around you to stay positive, to find new ways to bond, perhaps for a common thread. The commitment to a common thread brings individuals together, honoring their loved ones, and fostering strength, love, and commitment for the common thread.

Perhaps they can rally to create a new way to honor their loved one by creating a new non-profit, for example. The underlying belief is that the spirit of the loved one energizes those left behind and can create a positive impact on the "new normal" as a result of the change.

I am eternally grateful for the commitment that I can speak and feel my loved ones with me at any time and the conviction that I will see them again. I am glad that the knowledge and empathy I have are in alignment with my faith. I thank the Lord for gracing my path with amazing people, experiences, and an overwhelming sense of love. My daughter Susie possessed thankfulness for what she had in life and the chance for an afterlife where she can journey along with us here on earth and welcome us in the future. The thought of that embrace warms my heart and makes me smile.

In Susie's honor we created the nonprofit Susie Q's Kids, Inc. www.susieqskids.org, to create comfort bags (Q bags) to brighten and inspire the lives of children and young adults "one comfort bag at a time."

Roadmap to Self Help and Discovery Key Takeaways:
- ❖ Embrace your spiritual beliefs, know you and your loved ones are not experiencing punishment.
- ❖ Attend services, journal, meditate, whatever it takes to connect on a spiritual level to heal.
- ❖ Find a path to channel your time, volunteer, inspire, and help others, and give back.

Express your emotions:
Whether you believe in God or not, find the solace in your spiritual well-being, that place of inner peace. Channel your time to form a new outlook. What activities can help you bring peace?

_____

_____

_____

_____

_____

_____

_____

What is your action plan?

_____

_____

_____

EIGHT
DEALING WITH THE 'WHAT-IFS'

The what-ifs are the backbone of our grief. They tend to break us, to challenge our core with their devastating scenarios. According to WYG, when a person dies, you are not only robbed of their physical presence in the here and now, but you (and they) also lose the chance to spend your tomorrows together. Your life after their death becomes filled with thoughts of "if only," "we should have", and "I wish."[23]

We have to learn to give ourselves a break. The only way we can truly move forward is to forgive ourselves for our perceived slights, indifferences, and faults. If we can understand why it is important to forgive ourselves, we can begin to challenge our negative thoughts. Much of the time our actions could not change anything and if they could, who knows what the future outcome might have been or how different life might have been. If we had gotten there in time, perhaps life would have been in a hospital bed in a vegetative state. We must understand that it was their time to move on to the next step of their journey and ours as well. You did what you possibly could; it was beyond our capability to change the circumstances or events of their death. Our loved ones are no longer in physical or emotional pain. We must cherish and rejoice in this fact and focus on their happy times.

Don't blame yourself for making tough decisions. Instead of focusing on what-ifs which are not productive to your healing and cannot be changed, concentrate your thoughts on what was and what you did do.

I have added some here. You can list your what-ifs and then the "what was and what you did do." The exercise can be very eye-opening and healing (thanks to my therapist KT for guiding me). I hope it provides you with a different perspective to consider.

> WHAT IF?
> GIVE YOURSELF A BREAK.
> HONOR YOUR LOVED
> ONES, LET YOUR PASSION
> AND PURPOSE RE-EMERGE,
> AND LIVE CHERISHING
> THEIR MEMORIES.

> "TO LIVE IS THE RAREST
> THING IN THE WORLD."
> OSCAR WILDE (GOOD
> READS, N.D.).[24]

1. "What-if" doesn't matter… because we did, and it felt good. We loved her.

   a. We were present in her life. We celebrated with her, we cried, we laughed, we supported, we were always proud of her, and she knew it. We didn't have to say it again, we lived it with her. No matter what we might have said, there would always be that "one more" or "what-if."

2. "What if" we had been there? But we were there her whole life. We loved her.

   a. Regardless of her last moments, she knew we loved her. She experienced our love throughout her whole life. Even in those moments when we may have parented her, she knew it was for her best. Even if we had not been there with her in her last moments or she could not recognize us due to her medical state, she knew how much we loved her.

3. "What if" we hadn't spent enough time with her? But we did in good and bad times, always with love, understanding, caring, and hope. We loved her.

   a. We afforded her the space she needed as a young adult, although we were there to help and support her. We understood her desire to not see her as the "sick kid" in defining her, as it was not who she was, and she knew that we loved her.

4. "What if" we hadn't taken time to travel and enjoy life? But we did and had fun—treasured memories to last us a lifetime. We loved her.

   a. We took trips and planned a celebration to go on a cruise a year in the future, although we were unsure if she would be able to attend. She did shortly before her death. We enjoyed ourselves tremendously, making beautiful memories, and forgetting the future for the moment. She laughed and enjoyed herself and us. She knew that we loved her.

5. "What if" we hadn't loved her enough? But we did and it was truly awesome. She was truly a treasure. We loved her.

   a. How could we not? She was cherished even in the womb. There was a chance she would not be born. I was on bed rest with two infants at home. She arrived with a smile and smiled her entire life even when living with pain. She was thankful for us and told us often that "we were amazing, and she loved us and was forever grateful for us". She asked her Daddy Joe to adopt her as an adult. She was loved and loved us.

6. "What if" we had been sillier? But we were. We wore silly hats to celebrate, we retell funny stories. We loved her.

   a. She would tell stories about our silly birthday celebrations and laugh. A favorite was her Dad Joe eating dinner with a purple star on his head and wearing it as he walked into the piano bar. The pianist said, "Look at the guy walking in with a star on his head." All heads swiveled and he laughed when he recognized his family and friends in attendance.

   b. We went to the comedy shows; the comedian could be heard to say, "This is going to be easier than I thought," as Susie belly-laughed in the audience. Silly is fun, contagious, and good for the spirit. We loved and laughed together.

7. "What if" our home wasn't the welcome spot for everyone? But it is. Everyone gathers there—so much family and friends, she loved it. We loved her.

   a. Our home was always where the friends gathered, where the pool attracted company, where the love, laughter, and good times abounded, where the food never ran out, and where everyone felt welcome regardless if they were an ex, current family member, friend, or new acquaintance. She was at the center of it, her friends still come (Amber, Danni, April, Janelle, Haley, Jaime, Becky, Channing, Natalie, Lindsay, Theresa, Marcus, to name a few) and visit feeling welcomed and loved. She loved it and all of us.

8. "What if" we had processed the adoption paperwork? But paperwork is not necessary. She is ours.

   a. We understood that her health impacted her processing the necessary legal documents. She spoke her desire for Joe to become her legal dad and we cherish the sentiment involved in the asking. She and all the siblings were adopted the day we both said, "I do." We involved them in the wedding itself and the life that followed. She is our daughter and we love her.

9. "What if" we had taken responsibility for everything? But we couldn't. She was an adult and it was her responsibility. She tried, she cared. We loved her.

    a. She was like any independent young person wanting her independence but also basked in the love and care of her parents, family, and friends. It was hard to move home, but she knew home was where she could get the love, comfort, and care she needed. She felt our love and care.

10. "What if" we knew she was anxious and depressed? But we did. We helped her through it many days. She tried, she cared. We loved her.

    a. When the discussions led to the "whys," she would be frustrated and sad. She promised not to take her own life just for us to never know the pain of not being able to do enough. In the end, we let her know it was OK to go. She knew we loved her, and she felt the love and release that we would be OK. Her biggest fear was how we would be in her absence. A true caring person to the end and beyond, so loving, so loved.

11. "What if" we had forced attention she didn't want? But it was her life, we respected her. She loved, she cared, and we honored her. We loved her.

    a. We could have forced her to stay in our home during her adult life, but it would have crushed her formidable spirit. Instead, we let her live to the best of her ability, experiencing the world and sharing her spirit with others. She was loved.

12. "What if" we had argued with the doctors? But we did. She was in pain and she knew it. She would never have been pain-free. It was time to let go. We loved her.

   a. The doctors tried; the system sucked. Even if they had done something different, even if she had not gotten an infection, she would never be pain-free. We need to release that negative "what if" and concentrate on "what if we did something positive in her honor," so we created our non-profit, Susie Q's Kids, Inc., to help others as she helped others in life.

13. "What if" I had never birthed her; she would never have had all that pain? But she was a treasure worth all the pain we are suffering now with her passing—it is worth every moment that we had her with us. We loved her.

   a. Don't be ridiculous, she was the epitome of love, laughter, and a desire to be the best and loved helping her family, friends, and those who were in need. So, loved.

14. "What if" we waited a little longer to end her life? But we shouldn't, she didn't want it—she tried, she cared, we promised. We loved her.

   a. If we had left her on life-support machines, we could have uttered we loved her longer, hugged her more, told her again how much we loved her. We promised to let her go, just as she fought hard her entire life. We had to honor her wishes as those "one mores" would have led to more "one mores." We did the right thing.

15. "What if" her pain was for nothing? But it wasn't. She loved, she cared, we loved her, we cared, we celebrate her with fond memories and good deeds in her honor. We keep her alive in our minds and hearts by helping others as she did in life. We loved her.

     a. She loved life whole-heartedly. We should never doubt her thirst for life, her commitment to us, and her pleasure at loving or being loved. She is awesome!

Roadmap to Self Help and Discovery Key Takeaways:
- ❖ Don't blame yourself for making tough decisions. Instead of focusing on what-ifs which are not productive to your healing and cannot be changed, concentrate your thoughts on "what was and what you did do."
- ❖ What-if doesn't matter... because we did, and it felt good. We loved our loved ones.

Express your emotions:
Remove blame, create your list of what if and what I/we did statements. Share your pain and heal with new relationships, new processes, new reflections of your impact on how others respond.

_____

_____

_____

_____

_____

_____

What is your action plan?

_____

_____

_____

Express your emotions:
Follow my path. Make your own list of what-ifs and then "what was and what you did do." When put in this perspective, I was able to release some guilt. I hope you find it releasing.

WHAT IF? GIVE YOURSELF A BREAK.
YOU DID YOUR BEST.

What-if _____
But I/we did: _____

What-if _____
But I/we did: _____

What-if _____
But I/we did: _____

What-if _____
But I/we did: _____

What-if _____
But I/we did: _____

What-if _____
But I/we did: _____

What-if _____
But I/we did: _____

What-if _____
But I/we did: _____

What-if _____
But I/we did: _____

What-if _____
But I/we did: _____

What-if _____
But I/we did: _____

What-if _____
But I/we did: _____

What-if _____
But I/we did: _____

What-if _____
But I/we did: _____

What-if _____
But I/we did: _____

What-if _____
But I/we did: _____

What-if _____
But I/we did: _____

What-if _____
But I/we did: _____

What-if _____
But I/we did: _____

Roadmap to Self Help and Discovery Key Takeaways:
- ❖ What If? Give yourself a break. You did your best, consider "But I/we did" statements.
- ❖ Know your loved ones would not want you to be sad, to agonize, or retreat from living.

Express your emotions:
What are your What Ifs? How can you look at them alternatively? What did you do? How can you change your perspective? How would your loved ones want you to embrace living?

_____

_____

_____

_____

_____

_____

_____

_____

What is your action plan?

_____

_____

_____

NINE
COPING WITH YOUR CRAZY FEELINGS FOLLOWING YOUR LOSS

N one of us is the same. We are all grasping to come to terms with our "new normal," which has what could be considered "crazy" notions involved. Everyone is experiencing the loss in different ways, at different levels, and in their own personal ways.

> If ever a rationale for temporary insanity was needed, one could certainly be found among the range of reactions and emotions associated with grief and loss--*shock, numbness, sadness, despair, loneliness, isolation, difficulty concentrating, forgetfulness, irritability, anger, increased or decreased appetite, fatigue or sleeplessness, guilt, regret, depression, anxiety, crying, headaches, weakness, aches, pains, yearning, worry, frustration, detachment, isolation, questioning faith—to* name a few. [25]

Trying to understand our emotions is important to our self-care. Understanding the reactions are normal and you are not alone, may allow you to address your emotions in a healthier and more positive manner.

Understandably, many will find it hard to acclimate to these emotions. One day you're walking along like normal and the next day you feel like an alien has invaded your body; your actions and reactions have become totally unpredictable and confusing. In search of something familiar you look to your primary support system, your family and friends, but they seem changed as well; some avoid you, some dote on you, some are grieving in ways you don't understand, and some are critical of the way you are handling things. Everyone is searching for the new normal. [26]

Keeping things in perspective seems impossible when the loss rocks your world to the core. Trying to add some consistency to your life, establishing partners to contact when you are on the brink of despair, and finding healthier ways to get through the day will make your "new normal" a kinder one.

You know you will never be the same and you begin to accept that you must integrate your loved one and your experiences and continue to live...a little bit wary, a little bit wise, and a little bit crazy. [27]

The life before you lost your loved one had a purpose. You had a routine: work, school, family obligations, and so forth. Afterward, everything is in flux. Your schedule is in disarray, you worry about yourself, others, your loved one, and how will life ever be normal again. It won't; you and those who knew your loved one and you have changed as a result of your loss.

As you progress through the different stages of grief, you will waver in and out of creating that 'new norm' as will those around you. What triggers you might not trigger someone else. How you respond may force others to address it and bring forward differing perspectives. Life, as you all knew it had changed forever.

What you find essential post-loss can be very different from before your loss. It may drive you crazy as you deal with the fallout. People may avoid you choosing to refrain from having to deal with the sense of loss as it makes them uncomfortable, and it is their way of coping. We must learn to read others and make tough decisions in dealing with them; perhaps feeling free to discuss your loved one, refrain from bringing up the subject with them, or ending relationships that are counterproductive to our health. Remember, you are in charge; you must do what is best for you to adapt as your well-being matters most. You matter!

YOU MATTER. NEVER UNDERESTIMATE YOUR VALUE.

Time and patience will provide a sense of recovery. The pain will subside as you become healthier in your healing process. It will never go away; it may be less debilitating all the time, but you must realize that it can take you down at any time because it never goes entirely away. You may have relapses as a situation can bring you back to that overwhelming sense of loss and pain. However, the time to recover from them will become shorter. You will implement new ways to cope,

YOUR GRIEF WILL TAKE YOU ON A JOURNEY OF CHANGE.
IT IS A REFLECTION OF THE PRICE OF THE LOVE YOU SHARED.
CONTINUE ON THE PATH TO YOUR NEW NORMAL AS IT IS A PASSAGE, NOT A DESTINATION.

to remember them, and to honor them—and most important—to live again without them physically but always with you spiritually.

Roadmap to Self Help and Discovery Key Takeaways:

❖ The life before you lost your loved one had purpose, find your new purpose, and focus your energy on it thus aiding in your healing.

❖ Remember, you are in charge; you must do what is best for you to adapt as your well-being matters most. You matter! You matter. Never underestimate your value.

Express your emotions:

What can you do to reinforce your own perception of your value? Find your new purpose, what honors your loved ones and is good for you. Do you recognize those individuals who are good for your well-being? Those individuals who compromise your grief recovery process?

_____

_____

_____

_____

What is your action plan?

_____

_____

_____

Sharing with Others and Socializing

As you traverse the road to recovery, there are certain people, places, and times that will serve as triggers. The worst part of mourning in my opinion, is knowing our loved ones will not experience these, that we will miss them forever. It is incredibly unfair and painful, and you mourn not only what was but what will not be. We must learn to survive and can do so by involving others and continuing to talk about our loved ones.

Some triggers may be attending graduations, weddings, funerals, births of babies, reunions, birthdays, anniversaries, family gatherings, their birthday, their heavenly birthday, Mother's Day, Father's Day, and others.

Make a plan to handle them. In the first year, I found the mental agony leading up to the day was worse than the actual day. I surrounded myself with those who would mourn with me and also celebrate the occasion. Those are the people who would understand my need to have a moment and always be supportive with a kind word, hug, or gesture. In that first year, there are so many firsts.

The reality of the second year is that I survived the firsts, and although sad, I will survive the others as life continues for us all. My second Christmas season was also harder than the first. I felt more emotionally numb than in the first year. In speaking with other bereaved parents, I have concluded that they might always be hard as the years progress. Perhaps my grief moments may be just as intense, but my ability to spring back will increase.

Roadmap to Self Help and Discovery Key Takeaways:

❖ As you traverse the road to recovery, there are certain people, places, and times that will serve as triggers. Be aware and create options for dealing with them.

❖ We must learn to survive and can do so by involving others and continuing to talk about our loved ones, recognizing those triggers and avoiding them, or embracing them with the agony and pain of the realization they are gone but with you in spirit.

Express your emotions:

What are your triggers? How do you socialize and embrace or avoid your triggers? How can you be more inclusive allowing yourself to express your feelings? What measures can you take to improve your ability to grieve and adjust? Share your thoughts.

_____

_____

_____

_____

What is your action plan?

_____

_____

_____

A MOMENT

How to cope and set boundaries.

Let others know when you are having a moment, to let you have that good cry in private or public. It lets others know your pain; perhaps they can help you out of the moment. It's important to understand they cannot fix you, but they can support you with a kind word, gesture, or silence. You need to set the stage.

IT IS HEALTHY TO TAKE YOUR MOMENTS WHEN NEEDED.

My daughter Dusty thought she was doing a good thing by letting everyone in the house know I was outside crying in the garden one day. Although I told her I was fine, that I just needed a moment, she told mom. Others came to fix me or cheer me up. Later, I explained to Dusty and everyone that I need my "moments," my own space to deal with my grief.

After that, they left me alone with the intention that I would reach out if I needed human contact. Other days, I need compassion. It is my moment. Make sure you set your boundaries and act accordingly.

Another time my siblings might get a phone call where I say, "just talk, I need to keep from going down the grief rabbit hole of despair." The act of talking, sharing a memory, or talking about something funny could break the spell of heart-wrenching despair and let me move on sad, but not in utter despair. Find your avenue. Let others know if they get that call it might only take a minute or two, or perhaps be a "drop everything" lunch. Just ask them to be there as you are in a world of hurt at that moment in time and want to avoid hours or days of clawing out of the rabbit hole of despair.

Roadmap to Self Help and Discovery Key Takeaways:

- ❖ Take a moment. It's important to understand others cannot fix you, but they can support you with a kind word, gesture, or silence. You need to set the stage.
- ❖ It is your moment. Make sure you set your boundaries and act accordingly.
- ❖ Establish your call list for when you need help to avoid the rabbit hole of despair.

Express your emotions:

Share what a "moment" is and how you want people to respond to your expression of grief. Make your call list and let them know its purpose; stay out of the rabbit hole of despair—call them!

What is your action plan?

REACH OUT TO OTHERS

Create dates with your friends and loved ones on a daily, weekly, or monthly basis. Talk freely and listen as your family and friends are dealing with their trials. They could need you to listen, to coach, to mentor, and to just be there. Make it a mutual sharing of what is going on with you, permit them to share stories and memories freely, and for them to share with you. After all, relationships are built on mutual compassion and communication.

Those scheduled dates saved me (thanks to my husband, family, my friends, and my therapist KT, and doctor JF for guiding me). I recommend everyone take advantage of them. We all get lost in our own lives. These dates give us a break and remind us we are not only spouses, moms, dads, parents, friends. They allowed me to cry and talk freely in the beginning and then allowed me to be there for my friends to celebrate their successes and happy moments, to lend an ear or shoulder in their sorrowful or sad moments, and to get together and laugh and talk about everything and nothing. God gave us friends for a reason. Don't go it alone. Don't bottle it up inside: talk it out, cry at the injustice, live, which is exactly what your loved ones would want for you.

Roadmap to Self Help and Discovery Key Takeaways:
- ❖ Make dates, make phone calls, socialize, and learn to live your new norm.
- ❖ God gave us friends for a reason. Don't go it alone. Don't bottle it up inside: talk it out, cry at the injustice, live.

Express your emotions:
Create a list of people to call, old and new. Establish your meet-up dates. Start speaking freely and living again. They may need you as much as you need them.

_____

_____

_____

_____

_____

_____

_____

_____

_____

What is your action plan?

_____

_____

_____

SHOW-AND-TELL DAYS

Other opportunities for sharing involve what I call "show-and-tell days" where you share with your physician (thanks JF), therapist (thanks KT), family, friends, and associates (you all know who you are). It could be something sentimental that you found, or a recent gift (my daughter Angela made a blanket of Susie's Lions gear, T-shirts, and hoodies, priceless), or a group setting like the Bereaved Parents of Macomb County where we share our experiences on their birthday and heavenly birthday. It allows us to speak freely, share our emotions, and lets others see there is hope and healing happens. Be open to sharing.

During our Bereaved Parents Group meeting, we have brought pictures, gifts, items of importance to give others a glimpse of our child to show how much they meant to us and still do. My daughter Angela took all of Susie's Lions jerseys, shirts, and memorabilia and created a double-sided queen size quilt for me. It is priceless. I get to wrap up in Susie's warmth and remember all the good times we shared, laughing and crying at the Lion's antics. I shared my quilt with the group; they understood its importance.

I visited my therapist KT weekly. In the beginning, she asked me to bring something to share as a way to open dialogue and discussions. Over the course of my treatment, I brought some of those people most important in my life with me to demonstrate therapy was good and allow my therapist KT to get a grasp of me from another perspective (my husband, my mom, my mother-in-law, daughters, and grandkids). She laughed and said I was the first to refer to my family members as "show-and-tell." Do whatever it takes to share your story and heal.

Roadmap to Self Help and Discovery Key Takeaways:

❖ Do whatever it takes to heal. Show and tell days are simply items to start a dialogue and let the other person(s) know the importance of the memory.

❖ Involve others in your recovery. If attending therapy, take a significant other with you.

❖ Share personal treasures with others, it can be rewarding to talk about their importance.

Express your emotions:

It is hard to express, sometimes an item can spark the dialogue. How can you incorporate them into your sharing with others? What would you take to show-and-tell? What are you thankful for? Who might you take to therapy to aid you in recovery?

_____

_____

_____

_____

_____

What is your action plan?

_____

_____

_____

HELP OTHERS

Try to find ways to help others and yourself. By allowing others to share, by listening to them and by being aware of their pain, it may lead to nurturing that is helpful for both of you. When we look for the beauty that surrounds us, we must strive to understand our value and the value of others. Only then can we begin to heal. What do these people need, how does your grieving affect them? Even in our grief, we don't want to hurt others, intentionally or unintentionally. Try to be mindful of their needs and your own. If you are not in a good spot, call someone else to aid them. Make a follow-up call later.

Be receptive. When you hear others in pain, reach out. When someone shares their pain, listen.

Watch others. Does something they do to grieve resonate with you? If so, reach out to them to do it together. Ask them questions to learn how and why, ask for their help. Just as important, reach out to those who you have lost contact with. Set up dates to talk or meet. Those who loved your loved one: reach out and follow them on Facebook, keep an interest in their lives. Your contact may help them with their grieving and be that nurturing and positive connection to you as well.

During my daughter's long illness, I pushed friend visits to the side, trying to stay afloat with the situation. After Susie's death, I realized I needed my friends, I missed them. By taking the initiative, it allowed groups of us to gather together and keep in touch, a positive from the loss. Others meet one on one, also a good approach to rekindling long-lasting friendships. I also created new relationships with those suffering themselves, another positive result from our loss.

Keep in contact with your loved one's friends. They feel lost, and your kind words of encouragement may improve their mental health surrounding their loss.

I realized that my daughter's friends were floundering as well. By setting up lunch dates, pool dates or reaching out by phone, email, or Facebook, I kept in touch with them. I allowed them to share their memories, regrets, and accomplishments with me, their adopt-a-mom. I also feel connected, enjoy their friendships, and know my daughter would have wanted it no other way. A special thanks to April.

One such pool day, when all the girls came to talk and gather, felt like the first normal day following Susie's death. The stories flowed and she was talked about lovingly, laughter filled the air, just like in life.

Roadmap to Self Help and Discovery Key Takeaways:
- ❖ Shared stories can lead to acceptance that we are not alone, we all have a story.
- ❖ Being empathic to others, listening, and being receptive can create a foundation for mutual acceptance and healing.
- ❖ Make time for your friends, your loved one's friends, and new friends, creating a safe environment to talk and share your feelings.

Express your emotions:

How can you help others and yourself at the same time? Have you lost contact with some of your friends? Rekindle the relationship with a phone call or email. Are there people important in your loved one's life that you can help, that can help you by sharing stories about them? Be empathetic. Make the connection for a dinner night at the house or a restaurant.

_____

_____

_____

What is your action plan?

_____

_____

_____

MENTAL HEALTH ISSUES

It is everyone's commitment to and awareness of mental health issues that can aid us in suicide awareness and prevention. By being conscious of the mental health of others, we may be able to prevent someone from the overwhelming sense of depression that leads to suicide. When raising awareness for dealing with and recognizing mental health issues, we could contribute to getting someone the help they need by letting them know they are not alone and that we care. Be conscious of their cries for help, be vigilant in your response. Be an advocate for someone on the cusp of mental health issues.

We don't need to lose anyone else to suicide. In many cases, those who attempted suicide state they saw no way out. They felt it was best for them and those they loved. I am not a suicide counselor but would recommend that we have discussions with others that suicide is not the answer, you and others will forever be missing a piece of themselves, a portion of their heart, and will mourn the loss of a loved one. Express how much their parents, siblings, spouses, children, nieces, nephews, other family members, and friends love them. Consider participating in a suicide awareness walk so you and your loved ones can support others but learn first-hand the devastation of family and friends left behind, the pain they experience. Perhaps, it will make you or your loved one think first and ask for help.

All of them will feel the pain of their loss which will alter their lives forever. Share how much your life has changed at the loss of your loved one, whether by suicide or not, you and everyone they knew has a 'new normal.' Some cannot bounce back from the loss and have delved into a deep depression.

My daughter suffered from chronic pain her entire adult life, she missed many things a young adult should have experienced, she hid her pain and withdrew not wanting to be that poor sick kid. We talked about suicide and she said she had thought about it. The pain and despair were that bad. I shared that if she tried her best, and I did my best to help, we would get by. If the Lord decided her journey was to end, I would not want to let her go but would honor her wishes for no life support parameters. Then the decision was in His hands, and we would have both done what we could.

When she lay on her death bed, I told her it was time. She had kept her promise to me to do all she could in life, that we would all be OK, and we loved her so much, but it was time to move on. We withdrew life support, and a sense of peace surrounded her as she took her last breath and she was gone. (This act was so easy to make as she made known to us her wishes but so incredibly hard wanting to keep her).

Speak with your loved ones. What do they want, do they want to be on life support, be organ donors, be buried or cremated? It makes the decisions a little easier knowing what they wanted even if it conflicts with what you wanted?

You must know we are worthy of being loved, your families and friends need you, you deserve to enjoy those ordinary and extraordinary moments with others, you deserve the love, hugs, tears, laughter, and kisses from good relationships, you are worth it, and you should not inflict a lifetime of pain and sorrow from suicide on those you love! Hang in there, get the help and support you need.

Roadmap to Self Help and Discovery Key Takeaways:
- ❖ Be an advocate for someone on the cusp of mental health issues.
- ❖ Suicide is not the answer to mental health issues. Raise awareness that help is available for yourself or others. Don't let the pain impact everyone left behind that misses them.
- ❖ Speak with your loved one and understand their wishes and share your own regarding life support, organ donation, burial, and cremation.

Express your emotions:
Understand your emotional health and well-being and that of your loved ones is important. What are their wishes regarding life support, organ donation, burial, or cremation? What are you doing to prevent suicidal thoughts in yourself or others, be aware—seek help, if needed?

_____

_____

_____

What is your action plan?

_____

_____

_____

Young Family Members

Young family members have limited memories of their loved ones. They observe how comfortable you are about speaking about them, about sharing your memories and likes with them, and about making new and different types of memories or associations. Talk about them freely and often daily, keep them and their story fresh and ongoing. Show them pictures and reiterate stories about how they loved them and what they liked to do with them. Encourage them to understand their loved ones in heaven adore them. They are always with them; their presence surrounds them. Give them something special of their loved ones, a necklace, a piggy bank, a cup, a scrapbook.

With my grandchildren, we talk about them positively. When Susie passed, the kids would run to the coffin, rub her arm, and say, "We love you," and off they would go. Occasionally, I might make a statement about Susie liking something and reinforce her involvement with them or say a particular cloud looks beautiful, maybe because Susie is smiling at us from it. Tell them stories.

While taking pictures at my grandson Brandon's birthday I said, "Strike the Susie pose (two thumbs up and a big grin)." She is always with us; her love surrounds us. When we look at new pictures with thumbs up, we are reminded that she was with us in thought. (See Appendix C for the link to our Thumbs Up Revolution Facebook page).

Find ways to encourage the use of their name and reinforcement of their love. With my grandchildren, we do the following to speak her name: when taking a picture, instead of saying "cheese" we yell out "Susie;" when a dandelion puff flies by, we say "Hi, Susie and Keith (another family member);" when blowing bubbles, we would send them to heaven saying "Hi, Susie and Keith;" when coloring pictures, we add their names and hang them on the refrigerator, and during Christmas, we wrap presents from our loved ones as a special token of their continued love. Susie's ashes are held in a beautiful heart pendant hanging on my neck, and close to my heart, other hearts represent other loved ones. Their presence is always there. You need to make it happen.

Roadmap to Self Help and Discovery Key Takeaways:
- ❖ Talk about your loved ones freely and often daily, keep them and their story fresh and ongoing.
- ❖ Show children pictures and reiterate stories about how your loved one loved them and what they liked to do with them.
- ❖ Develop ways to encourage the use of their name and reinforcement of their love.

Express your emotions:
What can you do to include your loved ones in your daily lives? How can you ensure children remember or have a sense of their loved one? Share your thoughts and ideas with others.

_____

_____

_____

_____

_____

_____

What is your action plan?

_____

_____

_____

SOCIALIZE

Think about it: would your loved one want you to be sad all the time? Do what they would want you to do—live like you deserve! You will always remember your loved one but don't let their death define you. Remove yourself from the overwhelming sense of loss (yours and that of others). Take a break from the responsibilities of home and work and do something for yourself. Get out of the house, go for a walk, to the beach, schedule a card or game night, go to lunch or dinner with a friend, take in a movie, plan an outing to the theater, zoo, park, museum, or take a trip overnight, the weekend, or longer. Your loved one is encouraging you to move on, enjoy life, and remember them fondly.

When I think of a happy time with my daughter Susie, it was a cruise we took months before she passed. She was the daredevil on the jet-ski leading the pack smiling and laughing, although she shouldn't have with her medical issues. We enjoyed it anyway. Ten months later, my husband and I took a cruise with friends and planned only one excursion, to jet-ski as we did with her before. As I felt so close to her talking, crying, and laughing, I hit a wave that catapulted me into the air. I swear I could hear her say, "It's not your time, go back" as I did six somersaults in the air. When I hit the water, I broke six ribs. She was never a pain in the butt alive but was a pain in my side for months to follow. I felt so close to her, she always wanted us to travel and enjoy life, she was so proud of us. We will continue to travel and share special moments remembering her.

We are Lions fans, season ticket holders. She loved it. In her honor, I wear a custom jersey with #1 on front and Susie Q on the back. She is always there with us.

Create a date night every week with your significant other(s), don't let life interrupt it, keep it to protect your sanity and to keep your relationship positive and recharged. Thursdays are date night for my husband and I, rarely does anything infringe on it.

My husband and I have

DATE NIGHT. DEDICATE TIME TO EACH OTHER.

------

many pulls on our time but always spend Thursday evenings together with a meal, a comedy show, shopping, talking, or cuddling on the couch alone with a movie and a pizza. Thanks, everyone for supporting our initiative to stay closely connected. We talk, reminisce, and make new life plans knowing our mutual love is stronger for our time together. I love my hubby.

Roadmap to Self Help and Discovery Key Takeaways:
- ❖ Don't let your loved one's death define you. Remove yourself from the overwhelming sense of loss. They would encourage you to move on, enjoy life, and remember them fondly.
- ❖ Date night—dedicate time with your significant other as your time together is precious.

Express your emotions:
Assess your relationships, place emphasis on current ones, rekindle others, and let some go that are not supportive of your situation and journey (it's OK). How can you improve your social life? Plan a date night. Make your plans to stay connected and support each other.

_____

_____

_____

_____

_____

What is your action plan?

_____

_____

_____

UNDERSTAND YOUR TRIGGERS

Understand your triggers — which outings are useful and which others might be triggers for depression and deep feelings of loss. Know that you are the keeper of yourself. If the trigger is not right for you, then don't go. Send a card or gift or make a date for a quiet dinner celebration. Just listen to yourself. These types of outings can be triggers resulting many times from the overwhelming sense of loss that your loved one did not get to and will not experience them, or that it is just too soon for you to process them.

Remember these are special days to others: weddings, funerals, graduations, family gatherings, school trips. Be cognizant that your sadness could not only put you into a funk but may affect those having or sharing a special day. Make your excuses. If you decide to go, consider preparing yourself by letting someone know of your reservations. Give yourself permission to attend the ceremony only, or simply make an appearance and leave early.

My daughter Angela stood up in her best friend Becky's wedding shortly after Susie passed. She said, "You have to attend, mom, I can't do this alone and it might be the only time I walk down the aisle." It was difficult to attend. I sat in the back, shed many tears, but was present to support both girls. We gave a gift and made our regrets for not attending the gathering. Too much too soon, and the girls understood. My husband and I went out for a private dinner ourselves.

For funerals, we sent cards or messages with our regrets and condolences. Most people will understand. The wounds are too fresh. Listen to your triggers.

Prior to the ceremony of another wedding, I was sitting thinking of my girl never experiencing this joy. I went to silence my phone when a Facebook memory popped up; a message from Susie that I was the most amazing mom, and she appreciated all I did for her and everyone else. I left the church, cried, and met a woman who had lost her husband. We talked a moment or two about pennies and signs. I returned to the church in time for the ceremony with a sense of peace. Thanks for the message, Susie. Life goes on, but she and I know I will not forget her.

At her cousin Doug's wedding, I basked in the knowledge she would have been excited, dancing, laughing, and congratulating him and Aimee. The pride of new babies: Jack and Alyssa – Heinrick and baby, Lucas and Cheryl – Liam, and Doug and Aimee – Declen. The thought of her holding them and grinning from ear-to-ear made reckoning with her not getting married or having a child a little easier. She loved life and celebrating life events.

Understand the life you have here on earth challenges you and your loved one's spiritual form, and how you can make sense of it all. Give yourself a break.

Roadmap to Self Help and Discovery Key Takeaways:

- ❖ Give yourself a break. Your sadness is real. Be cognizant that your sadness could not only put you into a funk but may affect those having or sharing a special day.
- ❖ Make your excuses if you feel you can't attend, don't harbor guilt feelings.
- ❖ Go, consider preparing yourself by letting someone know of your reservations. Give yourself permission to attend the ceremony only or make an appearance and leave early.

Express your emotions:

Can you recognize your triggers? What are they? How will you prevent them from derailing your path to healing? Give yourself a break, don't go, take care of yourself!

_____

_____

_____

What is your action plan?

_____

_____

_____

TEN
GRIEVING IS VERY PERSONAL

G rieving is so very personal, there is absolutely no one fits all or one is better than another. How you grieve will impact how you come to terms with the loss, how you deal with life in general, and moving forward. Understanding that your loved ones may handle things differently is so critical. If you gauge their responses on how you grieve, you may be setting yourself up for pain and heartache by setting unrealistic expectations and putting undue stress on your relationships.

The death of someone close can be a life-changing experience. If you are the primary caregiver of someone you love, this experience can affect every aspect of your life for some time. It is natural to grieve the death of a loved one before, during, and after the actual time of their passing. Everyone experiences grief as an individual and the impact of grief depends upon the individual's past experiences with loss, their culture, their coping skills, belief system, faith, and life experiences." [28]

My daughter Susie experienced many medical situations over a long period. We had hard discussions about her health, her pain, her commitment not to commit suicide, her wishes on organ donation, and her desire for no extreme measures, no life support, and her unconditional love for life and her family. At the end, knowing this information along with her desires made the decision to withhold life support that much easier.

> A death is considered traumatic if it occurs without warning; if it is untimely; if it involves violence; if there is damage to the loved one's body; if it was caused by a perpetrator with the intent to harm; if the survivor regards the death as preventable; if the survivor believes that the loved one suffered; or if the survivor regards the death, or manner of death, as unfair and unjust. [29]

In our situation, Susie's death was ultimately from an infection of the body, her body had gone septic. It was untimely; is it ever really expected? We had friends suffer from the death of their children due to heart attacks, car crashes, suicide, overdose, and murder. How do you prepare? Their deaths are simply unthinkable. The challenge is learning to cope with the unthinkable.

> The problems set in when one individual fails to understand the pattern of grief in the other; they think of them as selfish or that they don't care enough, but it isn't about that – it's about different ways of coping. Grieving is an intensely individual and usually incredibly lonely experience, which can make it a particularly difficult time in a family, where a group of people will be going through something sparked by the same event but is in each case very different. The way to cope, says Julia,

is to be open in communicating how you are feeling to others in your family. The families that fare best are able to share their feelings openly. Death disrupts the complex and finely tuned balance in a family, so everything has to be reorganized – and being open helps with that process. [30]

Coping with grief is personal, some withdraw whereas others need to be surrounded by others. There is no best way, learn what works best for you and know it might differ in certain situations. Embrace your support system, let them know your secret trigger words so they can be alerted to your need for help. We all need help, don't be afraid to reach out for it.

The goal of grief support is not to stop the pain or forget about the loved one, but to help individuals live with the loved one's memory in a way that doesn't cause pain. [31]

Roadmap to Self Help and Discovery Key Takeaways:

❖ There is no one way fits all or one way is better than another when dealing with your grief. How you grieve will impact how you come to terms with the loss, how you deal with life in general, and with moving forward.

❖ Death is incomprehensible, we are never ready to say goodbye. There is usually always one more what if, could have, should have, would have—it is unfathomable to believe.

Express your emotions:

Do you understand that everyone's grief journey is individual? Family and friends grieve differently as well. Are you experiencing anxiety over how someone is grieving or appears not to be grieving? How does the manner of your departed loved one affect your ability to grieve?

_____

_____

_____

What is your action plan?

_____

_____

_____

GENDER DISCUSSION

The grieving process is different for men and women, for adults, teenagers, and children. The individual involved can cause more grief than others: an unborn child, a young child, an older child, a sibling, a best friend, a spouse or partner, or a parent or grandparent. The reason for the loss can also impact it: for example, old age, suicide, an unexpected car crash, a murder, an ongoing health issue, or other.

The loss of a child may be the hardest to endure. I believe that we should not compare individuals. Each person has experienced loss (even for the same loved one), and how they deal with it is highly personalized and should not be compared or discounted by others. Let's look at gender issues, the varying demographic age implications, and the reason for the death. Give yourself and others some slack; we are just trying to cope with our loss in our own way.

For Men

Men grieve differently than women and it is essential to understand the variances from how women grieve and are accepting of the differences remembering there is no right or wrong way to grieve.

> Men tend to be more comfortable attending to life changes by taking on new roles and responsibilities that result from the death of a loved one… so often they state that they know the story in their head, and they don't need to retell it. They tend to want to "fix it" and will rely on their resources – often keeping feelings and emotions to themselves. [32]

Observing my husband and son, I witnessed their quiet strength. They did not break down in buckets of tears over the past year-and-a-half and do not normally just bring up Susie or how they are coping. They respond when asked, and of course have their moments, but grieve differently from me. They embraced the need to fix things, to arrange things, to comfort in this way. They redid the yard, poured a concrete patio, reframed the garden walls, and made a beautiful memorial garden for the family to enjoy. They did work inside the house; their need was physical. Whereas, my need was to talk and talk and talk. They express their need as a solid strength of action and support.

I often asked how they were doing and if there was anything I could do. Their response was, "I am dealing with the loss." It was nice to have the support, but I wondered if they really were, as their approach was so different than mine. Not better or worse, just different.

In my grief support group, I heard from others as they shared their journeys. There seems to be that commonality of strength and need to fix things and not necessarily to talk about it with everyone all the time. I was glad to see the men share their feelings in this safe environment. They hurt just like the women, but differently.

Sometimes, relationships break down because one person cannot understand the variances in grieving. Please talk to each other. It is essential to have those shared moments together to talk of your loved ones. Remember, you are just grieving differently.

I give a shout-out to my husband Joe, my son Jim, and brothers Jim and Tom, my dad Basil, and all the men in my life who supported me on this grieving journey. You are so appreciated!

Roadmap to Self Help and Discovery Key Takeaways:
- ❖ We all grieve differently, there is no one best way to grieve. Respect it.
- ❖ Although men utilize different methods, they grieve just as deeply. Remember this.
- ❖ Men tend to talk less and keep busy doing things, taking action, protecting others.

Express your emotions:
Have you noticed a difference in how men and women grieve? Do you talk about it and respect the variances? How do the men in your life grieve? If you are a man, what would you like to share with those grieving with you? How do you express your grief and handle the loss?

_____

_____

_____

_____

_____

What is your action plan?

_____

_____

_____

For Women

Women are more apt to display their emotions than men do. The process of grieving varies, and we should be observant, so that hurt feelings don't occur because someone is grieving differently, or it appears, they don't care.

> Women, on the other hand, tend to be more emotional and will work on their grief by talking about it. They will tell their story over and over again because they say it helps them process and work through their grief. Women confide in friends, outwardly express their feeling and emotions and feel their way through grief. [33]

Well, this describes me! I have scheduled dates every week with my husband to encourage talking and respecting each other in our relationship. I planned monthly lunch and dinner dates with different groups of friends to talk, talk, talk. At first it was to talk of my girl, then it just became nights out where everyone has happiness, sadness, problems, or family to discuss, and friendship.

GIRLFRIENDS MAKE LIFE BETTER.

My elderly mother, Shirley, moved in with us following Susie's death. We have lunch dates, outings, and talks all the time to discuss our grief and love of life. She is a treasure. We recently took a ten-day vacation and cruise together to laugh, cry, and heal the losses we have endured. My in-laws Judy and dad Basil are constants in our life, we embrace life and share our grief positively in our time together.

I babysit my grandson Luke, and he fills the days with joy, a thirst and inquisitiveness for life, and a healthy understanding of death as we talk about Aunt Susie and his Uncle Keith all the time.

My family and friends are constants in our lives. They make it easier to talk about the past and the present and continue to live.

My husband and I embrace the need to change the scenery and the love we share; thus, we travel often, sometimes overnight trips and other longer vacations by ourselves or with other family members. We relish the fact that Susie loved our traveling and are glad we took a cruise just before her passing, a cherished memory.

My need to talk freely about Susie without always making others uncomfortable has resulted in embracing my writing and starting a non-profit in her honor, Susie Q's Kids, Inc. I am doing good by telling her story and the impact she had on us along with her need to give back, to help others. We hope this book helps people with their grief journey and the non-profit will aid children and young adults in their situations to know they are not alone, and that others care!

Roadmap to Self Help and Discovery Key Takeaways:

❖ We all grieve differently; women tend to be emotional, needing to talk more than men.

❖ Reach out and set dates to call or connect in person; we need to listen and share expanding on our feelings and being conscious of others.

❖ If you find it hard to talk, make a concerted effort to connect as it may be beneficial.

Express your emotions:

Have you created opportunities to connect with others? Do you talk freely about your loved one? Does it comfort you? Have you spoken with a therapist to enable you to talk through your feelings? Do you recognize the need in others to speak and provide them opportunities to do so?

_____

_____

_____

_____

What is your action plan?

_____

_____

_____

CHILDREN

An Unborn Child

When does life start? It can be a controversial subject. To a grieving parent, the loss of a child is an enormous sense of loss. The dreams for them are real, the "what ifs" drive us crazy (did we do something wrong), and for others, the loss is not tangible since the baby was not born or did not live beyond the birth, which may be incomprehensible to the grieving parents.

> It is estimated that one in every four pregnancies ends in a miscarriage, but though miscarriages are common they can still be highly traumatic for the couples who must cope with them. The aftermath of a miscarriage is often emotional, and it can take time for the individuals affected by miscarriage to work through their grief. Men in particular may feel confused about the miscarriage and how to proceed. Today there are many options for finding support and coping with miscarriage. [34]

How do men and women differ in the grieving of an unborn or a stillborn birth? How do they comfort each other? How can they console each other?

> Very often the men whose partners miscarry are particularly uncertain of how to proceed. Men may feel all of the same emotions in their grief over the lost pregnancy, but they may also have concerns for their partner's health and well-being as well. Some men may be reluctant to share their feelings, or even discuss the miscarriage, out of fear that it may upset their partner. Unfortunately, remaining silent may well upset the relationship. Making

time for intimate discussions should be high on the list of any couple following a miscarriage, so that both partners gain an understanding of how each is coping and what they can do to support each other. [35]

The Miscarriage Association (www.miscarriageassociation.org.uk), is also a source of information and support for individuals and couples affected by miscarriage.

I had three miscarriages with my first husband, who was not supportive. He just implied I should get over it! It? It is necessary to grieve the pregnancy and miscarriage. We mourn for the losses we endured, the "what-ifs," the "what would have been," and the "whys?" are never answered. Take your moments to remember those special angels.

> IT IS OK TO MOURN THE LOSS OF AN UNBORN BABY.

Never assume that those who had a miscarriage or stillborn are less pained than those who had a child born that lived for a short while or a lifetime. Death should not be compared; it is very personal. Mourn your loss and support those who have endured the pain of loss.

A Toddler and Babies

Toddlers and babies have not had the chance to live, the grieving for them recognizes all the lost opportunities they will not experience in life. Additionally, trying to find the right way to help young children mourn can be challenging for parents grieving the loss of loved ones.

At this young age, babies and toddlers don't have an understanding of death nor the language to say how they are feeling. However, they can definitely experience feelings of loss and separation and are likely to pick up on the anxiety or distress of close adults or others around them. [36]

Speak about your loved ones and share the stories with other young kids. Kids recognize the loss and want comfort as well. Take the time to ensure that you share stories about their loved ones and let them know they are with you simply in a different way. I share stories about my daughter with my grandchildren all the time. We talk about things that remind us of her like butterflies, finding a penny, or seeing shapes in the clouds. We celebrate her birthday with cake and friends and send balloon hellos to the skies. They get presents from her commemorating their birthdays or holidays like a new book with an inscription inside. Make it normal to speak about those loved ones gone too soon. They will be more comfortable sharing their questions and thoughts with you.

Roadmap to Self Help and Discovery Key Takeaways:

❖ The loss of a child is real, whether by miscarriage, a stillborn birth, those that live for a few moments, or those that had a chance to grow. Respect and honor your loss. It is real.

❖ There is a disruption of the normal life cycle as we should outlive our children, watch them be born and grow, and never feel the pain of their loss.

Express your emotions:

Did you experience a miscarriage or stillborn? How do you cope? Have you spoken with a therapist to express your emotions? Are you supportive of those who had a miscarriage or stillborn? Your child regardless of their age has left a void, talk about them and your feelings.

_____

_____

_____

_____

What is your action plan?

_____

_____

_____

Young Children

Just like babies and toddlers, the loss of a child is unfathomable. All the firsts, the dreams, and the significant events will never occur. Life as we knew it has disappeared. For the young children who have lost a significant loved one, the challenge to understand is even harder.

> Primary school children are still learning to understand death and can have some confused thoughts about it. They may think death is temporary, or that the person who has died may still feel things, such as coldness, hunger, or loneliness, etc. They may ask where the person is now and have blunt questions to ask about what happened to them and to their body. Explaining death to them is very important. [37]

My grandkids are very curious, and we often talk about their loved ones who have died. There are shelves in their homes with pictures, candles, urns, and angels that commemorate their lives. We have plants that need watering to signify life continues, we have memorial gardens where their presence can be found, and we have pictures and photo albums commemorating their lives. Look for pennies, butterflies, dandelion puffs, and be responsive to their quest for a connection. Be open, answer their questions to the best of your ability, let them know they can always talk to them, and to be open to their love and presence.

I've written a book, *Susie Q's Kids Positive Reflections: My Special Angel,* about the grief of a loved one addressing the questions my grandchildren asked about Susie. My hope is it helps them adapt to their loss.

Roadmap to Self Help and Discovery Key Takeaways:

❖ Children deal with their feelings not really understanding the reality, but that it's different.
❖ Find ways to talk about your loved ones with young children; reiterate memories and create new ones to keep their names and impact on their lives alive.
❖ Start new traditions to keep their memory alive, we hold our thumbs up in pictures.

Express your emotions:

How do you encourage the kids to talk about their loved ones? What situations encourage these discussions? Take the time to discuss them often. Use pictures and crafting to keep up the discussion and create new ways to remember them.

_____

_____

_____

_____

_____

What is your action plan?

_____

_____

_____

Teenagers

Losing a teenage child can be overwhelming, they have not had the opportunity to grow and become the young adults they have aspired to be. It can also be frustrating for teenagers that have lost a loved one as they understand death is inevitable, but it happens to others and can rock their young world.

> By adolescence, death is accepted as part of life, but it may not have affected a teenager personally yet. Their reactions may fluctuate between earlier age group reactions and reactions that are more adult. [38]

> Teenagers will often want to be more with friends than family as they seek support. They may find the intensity of emotion overwhelming or scary and not be able to find the words or ways to talk about them with others. They may want to feel they're coping, and be seen to be, but inside be hurting a great deal, or be putting their emotions on a shelf for a later time. [39]

My older grandchildren, Jakob and Brandon, remained quiet after the loss of their Aunt Susie and Uncle Keith. When asked, they would respond that they were OK. They were, however, open to memories shared and outings when we would recount good times from the past. We started a tradition that we place our thumbs up in a picture that allows us to think of them at the time, and in the future, when we look at the pictures, we will remember that they were with us in thought.

Roadmap to Self Help and Discovery Key Takeaways:
- ❖ Teenagers may find it difficult to express their feelings and how the loss is affecting them and their emotions and actions.
- ❖ Engage teenagers in discussing past experiences allowing them opportunities to talk.
- ❖ Start new rituals to embrace their feelings of love for them.

Express your emotions:
How can you entice your teenagers to talk or share memories? Consider continuing to do things they enjoyed together and then mentioning them. Talking about them keeps their memory alive. Be creative and make new rituals.

_____

_____

_____

_____

_____

What is your action plan?

_____

_____

_____

SENIORS

Seniors have been exposed to death as it is a typical path of aging. Many times, they are challenged with memory issues as they age, and the loss of a child or grandchild should not happen and can be unsettling for them to comprehend.

How do we experience grief and depression differently? To put it simply, grief often rides like a wave: A grieving person can usually find moments of levity inside the darkness, something to spur a smile or a moment of joy. Depression, however, often feels like being buried in a dark hole where no light comes through for extended periods of time. [40]

When an older person grieves, be gentle. Their existence may be upset. Their ability to watch others suffer the loss can be more than they can handle, and the loss can provide them with an unsettling sense of existence.

Listen attentively. Be a healing presence by being a good listener. Talking is a way of expressing grief. They may need to tell their story over and over; it helps them to process and accept the death. If they don't feel like talking, offer to sit with them in silence. Be understanding. [41]

Unfortunately, our senior connections may have experienced more loss. They may also be suffering from bouts of aging, memory loss or confusion, dementia, and Alzheimer's and tend to relive the loss or losses and retell the stories over and over. Be patient with them, let them talk, let them reminisce, let them honor those they miss, as they may also be suffering from their own fear of death or mortality.

My mom (92 years old) has lost so many family members. My challenge was that I was mourning my daughter, her first deceased grandchild. When I would have a moment, we would feed off each other. I had a hard time trying to console her for all her losses when I was caught up in the throes of my own loss. Time is a healer. It allowed me to say, "I can't fix you at this time," when necessary, and at other times it made me challenge my loss and console her.

The critical thing to understand is that we all mourn differently for specific individuals and situations. Just be there, be aware, and be honest in your approach. We can get through this all together. There is no right or wrong way to mourn.

Roadmap to Self Help and Discovery Key Takeaways:

- ❖ Be patient, the elderly normally experienced a higher exposure to loss based on their age.
- ❖ Let them reminisce. Don't correct them, listen to their stories, thoughts, and fears.
- ❖ Commiserate with them regarding their loss and be sympathetic.

Express your emotions:

Be patient with older family and friends. What can you do to make them more comfortable? An outing, a change of pace, or a heartfelt discussion? Listen and commiserate with them.

_____

_____

_____

_____

_____

_____

_____

What is your action plan?

_____

_____

_____

ELEVEN
RELATIONSHIPS

How Do Relationships Matter?

A Sibling

If you have been blessed with a sibling or two, you know the ups and downs of the relationship. The closeness the family bond can bring, the need for competition, and the need for supporting each other. You usually want to be there for life's good or bad moments as you truly feel connected and loved. Their loss can be devastating looking at what was and what will not happen together.

> Sibling relationships obviously vary in their degrees of closeness, love, and amicability. Some siblings may be thick as thieves, others wonder whether they're even really related. Regardless, siblings are our ties to family bonds. They have known us the longest. They understand our history and are the people with whom we have the longest-running jokes. They are our bridesmaids and our groomsmen. They are our children's aunts and uncles. They bail us out when we're in trouble, they loan

us money and then we loan it back. They are the most judgmental people we know. They are the most accepting and loving people we know. Siblings can never be replaced and when they are gone, we miss the hell out of them. [42]

Siblings are
Forever Friends
Attached
Heart to Heart

Understand that all those lifetime dreams and expectations are forever changed. All those special moments you want to or expect to share are gone forever. Although they might not be part of your wedding, you can especially remember them on that day. Perhaps they would have been the crazy aunt to your children, creating memories for your kids of their younger-day antics.

Be aware that their physical presence is missing, but they are always with you in your heart and mind. It is as if you can hear them laughing at your silly antics, giving a hug of encouragement, a slap at the head "what's up?" They are never far. Just talk to them out loud or in your head.

The sibling bond transcends life and death. Keep visual mementos and pictures to give you a physical presence.

Roadmap to Self Help and Discovery Key Takeaways:

❖ Their presence is felt consciously and unconsciously, a bond of strength, understanding, caring, and love. Embrace and relish it.

❖ Remember them lovingly and inspire your actions with their presence and influence guiding you as they are always around you.

Express your emotions:

Embrace your loved one's presence? Do you keep their memory alive in your approach to life? Let them inspire you? Give them a part of your special days as they are always with you in spirit.

_____

_____

_____

_____

_____

_____

_____

What is your action plan?

_____

_____

_____

A Spouse or Partner

We build spousal relationships on mutual caring and love for each other, to love and support each other, to strengthen families and friendships, and fulfill the need to live out your days together. When the dynamics change and your spouse leaves or dies, the foundation of who you are is upturned.

> When your spouse dies, your world changes. You are in mourning—feeling grief and sorrow at the loss. You may feel numb, shocked, and fearful. You may feel guilty for being the one who is still alive. At some point, you may even feel angry at your spouse for leaving you. All of these feelings are normal. There are no rules about how you should feel. There is no right or wrong way to mourn. When you grieve, you can feel both physical and emotional pain. [43]

Death and divorce are two events that should not happen to couples in love and committed to each other. I have experienced the pain and suffering of a divorce. I find the thought of losing my husband to death unimaginable. The loss of my daughter has made me realize the importance of others in my life. It reinforced the commitment to those relationships: scheduled dates, travels, talks, walks, movie nights, and cuddle time.

Take the time to appreciate the now so that when the unimaginable occurs, you have wonderful memories to cherish. You know you lived life to the fullest and showed your partner your love and commitment. To my husband, Joe, you are my rock! You are the rock of our family. We are forever grateful for your love, support, and friendship. Susie even asked you to legally adopt her shortly before she died, you have had such an impact on us. Whichever of us goes first, the other will find comfort in their spirit and warmth. Love you to the moon and back!

Roadmap to Self Help and Discovery Key Takeaways:

- ❖ All relationships are precious, and you should cherish them. Forget the small struggles and concentrate on their gift of love and support.
- ❖ Let your spouse/partner know you care, communicate, and spend time together. For those deceased, cherish those times together, the dreams, the goals, and try to live as you would have as a couple. Visit family and friends, enjoy an activity you both enjoyed, travel, and share your hopes, fears, laughter, and sadness with them through personal discussions.

Express your emotions:
What would you tell your spouse if they were still alive? If they are still alive, show them you care. Don't get caught up in the day-to-day doldrums; live life to its fullest. Show them you care, share your memories, and support each other in your grief.

_____

_____

_____

What is your action plan?

_____

_____

_____

A Parent or Grandparent

If a grandchild dies, the grandparent grieves twice: They grieve the loss of the grandchild while carrying the pain of their own child's suffering.[44]

Losing a child is just not the order of things. When we have children, we think we will grow old with them and never think that they will die before us. There are so many first, seconds, thirds, etc.,

> THE WORLD IS FULL OF LOVE WITH PARENTS AND GRANDPARENTS IN THE WORLD.

that will never happen, and the chasm of pain is so deep and unbearable. Time does make the despair somewhat easier, but the rabbit hole of despair can open up and swallow you at any time. Recognizing the triggers and having a good support team can make the loss somewhat more bearable. You should never beat yourself up for your sorrow, for experiencing painful moments, but you can learn how to react and manage the hard times.

For grandparents, the loss is not merely the loss of a grandchild but also of watching their child(ren) and their grandchildren's siblings and cousins in pain. Again, the reasonable expectation is that their children will outlive them, and when the order is disrupted, many emotions come into play. There is bargaining and anger that this happened, distraught emotions of loss, pain, and hopelessness that they cannot correct the situation. Be aware of their feelings and try to soothe their anger and distress at the situation. Remind them that their loved one would not want them to be in such pain and distress.

Roadmap to Self Help and Discovery Key Takeaways:
- ❖ Grandparents are hurt double in the death of their grandchild. They mourn their grandchild and all the dreams that are unable to occur. They also grieve the sadness and hurt their child is experiencing wanting to absorb some of their sorrow.
- ❖ Be supportive of grandparents; let them reminisce, share their sorrow, and grieve openly.

Express your emotions:
What triggers do you recognize? How can you work through them? How can you support other parents or grandparents? What gets you through the rabbit hole moments of depression?

_____

_____

_____

_____

_____

_____

What is your action plan?

_____

_____

_____

TWELVE
HOW THEY DIED

The circumstances of death can impact your grieving. It could be the result of normal aging, an unexpected incident, an ongoing illness, or medical situation, suicide, an accident, a murder or an overdose. Each type has their own set of emotions. No grief is the same for people experiencing the loss of the same loved one.

Death from Normal Aging

It is hard to watch the elderly and possibly yourself, deteriorate with time. Your mind, your actions, your ability to move and respond slow down, and your emotional state breaks down from the losses experienced physically, emotionally, and financially.

Human aging, physiological changes that take place in the human body leading to senescence, the decline of biological functions and of the ability to adapt to metabolic stress. In humans, the physiological developments are normally accompanied by psychological and behavioral changes, and other changes, involving social and economic factors, also occur. [45]

During periods of grief, the elderly not only mourn the loss of their loved one but also the sadness of previous losses. They worry about their mortality. Take the time to learn about their lives, listen to their stories, and be aware of their fears for the future. One day they will be gone, and you may suffer regret from not spending more time with them.

Roadmap to Self Help and Discovery Key Takeaways:
- ❖ During periods of grief, the elderly not only mourn the loss of their loved one but also the sadness of previous losses. They worry about their mortality.
- ❖ Death is inevitable, be patient with those aging and recognize changes in their mental and physical inability. This understanding will aid you in coping with their death or them dealing with the loss of their loved ones.

Express your emotions:
How can you address the subject of death with those aging around you? What can make them feel better? How can you aid them in sharing their stories or concerns? What can you do to help put them at ease?

_____

_____

_____

_____

What is your action plan?

_____

_____

_____

Death by Unexpected Circumstances

When death is unexpected, an accident, a murder, a suicide, a medical situation; it can be very traumatic. We question so much about the situation. Should we have foreseen it, could it have been avoided, did our actions play a part in the death of our loved one, are the authorities involved, will legal preceding ensue, has their body been recovered, is an autopsy required? What could, should, or would have happened if only.

Coping with the violent death of your loved one—by murder, accident, or suicide—is one of the most severe challenges anyone can face. If you and your family have experienced such a loss, you have my deepest sympathy. When the agony begins, it can be impossible to imagine that there is any way to ever find the slightest relief from your ordeal. On top of experiencing the natural pain of any loss, you find yourself particularly vulnerable to two of the harshest aspects of the grief process: self-punishment and chaos. [46]

The loss is unbearable by itself. The thought that you are ready for death is hard to imagine, as the what if or one more syndrome is usually present. Even if your loved one is sick like Susie was, I was not ready. But adding the unexpected tragedy element of loss finds the surviving loved ones at a loss. I have witnessed the loss debilitate them and their ability to grieve their loss positively.

The circumstances of sudden, violent death thrust survivors without warning, and often without any direction or adequate support, into a pool of torment where emotions batter and rage without mercy. At the same time,

you are often required to deal with unfamiliar responsibilities, unrealistic demands, and painful intrusions
(from the judicial system, the media, the medical world)
that result from the violent death. All of this creates a
high level of personal chaos and confusion. [47]

In my grief, I rallied against the injustice of Susie's loss,
but did not have to deal with blaming someone for a murder,
an accident, the justice systems, lawyers, autopsies, warring
family or friend's reactions, etc. If you find yourself in this
situation, please see a therapist to help you navigate the
warring emotions the circumstances present.

It is natural under such circumstances to try to make
sense of things, to grasp at something that will provide
order. One of the most common ways many survivors
seek to do this is by assuming guilt—to some degree or
another—for their loved one's death. Their thinking
goes, if only I had said something, or done something,
or recognized something, then this terrible loss would
not have happened. In other words, I had the power to
prevent my loved one's death and I did not do it. [48]

As discussed in an earlier section, give yourself a break.
Don't blame yourself for making or dealing with tough decisions or situations. Instead of focusing on what-ifs which
are not productive to your healing and cannot be changed,
concentrate your thoughts
on what was and what you
did do. Breathe and remember the good times, not the
death as that moment does
not define them.

> DEATH SHOULD NOT BE
> FEARED. YOUR LOVED
> ONES ARE AT PEACE.

199

Roadmap to Self Help and Discovery Key Takeaways:
- ❖ Breathe and remember the good times, not the death as that moment does not define them.
- ❖ The agony of the death is exacerbated by the unexpectedness of the situation, the guilt, the need to place some emphasis on the madness surrounding your loss, and the anger at those involved.
- ❖ On top of experiencing the natural pain of any loss, you find yourself particularly vulnerable to two of the harshest aspects of the grief process: self-punishment and chaos.

Express your emotions:
What feelings of guilt might you have? What power did you have to change the situation? How can you forgive yourself for these feelings of helplessness in the situation and moving forward?

_____

_____

_____

What is your action plan?

_____

_____

_____

Death from an Ongoing Medical Situation

From my daughter, I learned it is important to understand the wishes of our loved ones and to share our desires. We had financial and medical power of attorney forms completed for those for whom we had power of attorney. When we had to make decisions, regardless of our beliefs or wishes, we followed her desires.

My daughter Susie would call her immediate family from the pre-op room before any surgery and say a hello. Little did they realize she was calling to say goodbye just in case. As she would be wheeled away to surgery, I could hear her say to the nurse, "I have a do not resuscitate order on file, I don't want to live on life support." She made her wishes very clear.

> It is not unusual to experience guilt or shame for wishing it were finally over or feeling as though their loved one is already a memory instead of a still-living presence. They may agonize over what they should or shouldn't do regarding medical interventions and wish for a quick and final resolution that will relieve them of the painful burden of decision-making. Other commonly experienced reactions include hopefulness quickly countered by hopelessness, rage, denial, extreme anxiety, and deep depression. Throughout the time of anticipatory grief, it is crucial to seek and accept as much caring support as possible.[49]

Our daughter Susie had a lifetime of illnesses. We talked about death, her wishes, what scared her, but never really thought or wanted it to happen. We had a Do Not Resuscitate (DNR) order, had a will, discussed organ donation, burial versus cremation, all with the surreal belief that she would live a long life, certainly outlast her parents. When she became critical due to a complication and infection, we knew her wishes to remove life support. We made the right decision, although we did not want to. We wanted life as it was, but never to be again.

The night prior to her death, she told me to go to bed. "Mom, if you don't take care of yourself, you won't be able to help me or anyone else."

> TAKE CARE OF YOURSELF
> AS YOU MATTER.

It was easier for us to let her go when we had to make the decision the next day, she had made it easier for us to let her go. Not doing so, would have been wrong.

Roadmap to Self Help and Discovery Key Takeaways:
- ❖ Feelings that accompany illness and loss can include helplessness, hopelessness, rage, denial, extreme anxiety, and deep depression.
- ❖ Surround yourself with a good support system to navigate the feelings.
- ❖ Take care of yourself, you matter.

Express your emotions:
When someone has medical issues, take the time to learn their wishes as it will make your decisions somewhat easier. Who is on your support team, how can they help you?

_____

_____

_____

_____

_____

_____

_____

What is your action plan?

_____

_____

_____

Death by Suicide

When a person succumbs to suicide, they are not within their right frame of mind. In my personal belief, they are pained beyond comprehension. They can see no way to address the situation, they want the pain or depressive state to end, and they might feel that they are helping their loved ones burdened with their depression.

> When people are suicidal, their thinking is paralyzed, their options appear sparse or nonexistent, their mood is despairing, and hopelessness permeates their entire mental domain. The future cannot be separated from the present, and the present is painful beyond solace. [50]

Raising suicide awareness, being more observant of suicidal tendencies and statements, being more openly tolerant of discussions regarding suicide, and less judgmental may save a life or give another person hope. Once the suicide attempt takes place, we need to help the individual feel there is hope. If the suicide is successful, we still need to further the discussion to help prevent future suicides and attempts.

> After a suicide death, as with any other type of death, the bereaved may seek to make sense of what happened. However, in this instance they may find that many of their questions are either unanswerable or they lead to distressing conclusions (whether these conclusions are true or not). It is not uncommon for themes of personal blame to arise as the person questions their role in their loved one's suicide and what they could have done to prevent their death. Unfortunately, the bereaved may vastly overestimate their own role and the role of others (i.e. what family and friends did or didn't do), as opposed

to blaming things like mental illness which is quite often present. [51]

As the survivors, we must learn that we were not responsible. It was the decision of our loved ones. In most situ-

> CHOOSE LIFE. STOP SUICIDE. SAVE A LIFE.

ations, we could not have prevented the outcome. We may have tried or seen the signs but were unable to change the outcome. We must realize that their wish was not to hurt us or anyone else, but to be removed from the pain or confusion that overwhelmed them. Do not let their last moments define who they were. Remember them fondly, forgive them for any anger you may have, love them as you did in life as they still love you and meant you no harm!

The more we understand and talk about suicide prevention, perhaps we can help someone see an alternative. My efforts to reduce suicides and support their survivors include volunteering and donating financially to the American Foundation for Suicide Prevention (AFSP), including suicide prevention awareness material in my nonprofit comfort bags given to children and young adults, and participating as a Tragedy Assistance Program for Survivors (TAPS) peer mentor. (See Appendix D).

TAPS is a U.S. non-profit organization that provides care and support to families and friends grieving the loss of a member of the armed forces. By listening and supporting others, we make a difference, sometimes between life and death.

Roadmap to Self Help and Discovery Key Takeaways:

- ❖ When a person succumbs to suicide, they are not within their right frame of mind.
- ❖ As the survivors, we must learn that we were not responsible. It was the decision of our loved ones. In most situations, we could not have prevented the outcome.
- ❖ By listening and supporting others, we may make a difference, sometimes between life and death.

Express your emotions:

How did their death impact you? Do you blame yourself? How could you have changed things, most likely not. Talk about suicide, let those living know you care and that you are there for them. Your discussion might just be what someone else needs. Be there!

_____

_____

_____

_____

What is your action plan?

_____

_____

_____

Death by Car Crash/Accident

Accidental death is something that happens to someone else. Work accidents, building accidents, pedestrian accidents, car crashes all happen daily, they are not expected and thus are hard to wrap your mind around.

> Death through accident is usually a jarring experience. By their very nature no one expects accidental deaths and the fact that friends and family will not likely have had time to say goodbye can make these events even sadder. Whether it happens through road traffic accidents, accidents at work or in any other manner, accidental deaths are shocking, upsetting and can require those working through bereavement to find professional help in coping with their grief. [52]

Once the shock wears off, the questions persist. What could have been done to prevent the situation. Did our loved one know what was happening, was their pain, were they alone, did they ask for me? Why them and not me? Did the person responsible for the accident show remorse, was justice served? Did the legal system exacerbate the pain? So many questions why.

> It is normal to worry about if the person was in pain. Many survivors of accidents talk about not feeling anything as their body was in shock initially. Many family members and friends can't get the images of the violence out of their heads, whether or not they saw it happen. Many talk about visualizing the act step-by-step in their head like a horror movie. Some dream about such images. However usually what we imagine is often far worse. Some feel guilty that they should have been able

to save the person from death. If only you had known. You think if only you hadn't gone to work that day or out to dinner. Remember that no one can anticipate such a tragedy. Many loved ones wait for the murderer to get caught and brought to trial. Pass on any information you have to the police. [53]

Life is so tenuous; it can begin and end at any time. My friends have lost their kids in a car accident. The phone call or knock on the door is surreal, you can never prepare for that moment. Everything is normal one minute and upside down the next. The mind wants to know if they suffered, did they ask for them, were they alone, what were their last thoughts. The what-ifs drive you crazy, and the one more hug, kiss, or "I love you" never given drive you crazy.

The loss of your loved one is compounded by the anger surrounding the accident, the need for an autopsy, the legal battles, and the mental challenges surrounding the situation. The loss by itself is bad enough, but this added anguish and stress make it unbearable. Give yourself a break.

As the survivors, the questions and the regrets plague us. What if they had stayed home? You ask yourself if you had picked them up, if you had dinner at a later time, if you hadn't given them a car, so many "what-ifs." It was their time; they knew you cared and loved them. They loved you.

Roadmap to Self Help and Discovery Key Takeaways:
- ❖ Life is so tenuous; it can begin and end at any time. The loss of your loved one is compounded by the anger surrounding the accident, the need for an autopsy, the legal battles, and the mental challenges surrounding the situation.
- ❖ The loss by itself is bad enough but this added anguish and stress make it unbearable. Give yourself a break. It was their time; they knew you cared and loved them.

Express your emotions:
How can you support your loss or the loss of an acquaintance when it was not expected? Make a list of the words and events that you shared demonstrating you loved them so you can reflect on the fact that they knew you loved them, and they loved you!

_____

_____

_____

What is your action plan?

_____

_____

_____

Death by Murder

Why does one person take another person's life? What were they thinking and why my loved one? The questions are never ending.

One of the most difficult types of death to cope with is murder. The death is completely sudden and leaves family, friends, and communities shattered, feeling helpless and not knowing what to do. Sometimes the person is missing for a time and in this situation often people have two death dates that they remember. The first one is the date the person was found missing and the second when the body was discovered. [54]

The haunting questions exacerbate the loss: when they were listed as missing, when found, when not found, who is responsible, what is the rationale for the act, the deliberateness, the randomness, and the senselessness.

Normal reactions are anger, fear, confusion, and shock. It is one of the hardest things for a family to cope with. If you have suffered this loss, I am so very sorry that you are having to go through this. Many things that are common for families who have to deal with this tragedy are a feeling of not being safe. Many loved ones wonder what it was like for their loved one to have been murdered. Did they know they were going to die? What was she thinking about in those last moments? It is comforting to know that most likely it all happened so fast that the person had no time to think that she would die. [55]

Murder is just wrong, there is no right situation when it should occur. The individual murdered did not ask for this ending, it was no fault of their own. The family and friends left behind did not ask for this situation to occur. They love their loved one and cannot fathom the pain or fear they might have experienced, along with the loss of their company.

Similar to the loss of your loved one from an accident, this type of crime is compounded by the anger surrounding the murder, the need for an autopsy, the legal battles, and the mental challenges surrounding the situation. The loss by itself is bad enough, but this added anguish and stress make it unbearable that someone wronged your loved one on purpose. They determined that their life had no value or purpose, how wrong they were. Your loved one had a life and should have been given the right to live it without the interference of others. Their existence mattered.

Give yourself a break. As the survivors, the questions and the regrets plague us. What if they had stayed home, if you had picked them up, if you had dinner at a later time, if you hadn't gotten in an argument, they hadn't been in the wrong place or with the wrong people, so many what-ifs. It was their time; they knew you cared and loved them. They loved you.

It is essential to speak with someone professionally to address the many facets of emotion surrounding a murder of a loved one. They can help you through the range of emotions involved with this type of loss. Be there for family and friends, listen, and offer support and empathy as they deal with their emotions.

Roadmap to Self Help and Discovery Key Takeaways:

- ❖ Murder is just wrong, there is no right situation when it should occur. The individual murdered did not ask for this ending, it was no fault of their own.
- ❖ Give yourself a break. As the survivors, the questions and the regrets plague us. So many "what-ifs." It was their time; they knew you cared and loved them. They loved you.
- ❖ It is essential to speak with someone professionally to address the many facets of emotion surrounding a murder of a loved one.

Express your emotions:

It is important to get professional help. Have you contacted a professional? Have your family members? Perhaps, join a group therapy session for support from others that have shared a similar type of loss. Share your approach.

_____

_____

_____

What is your action plan?

_____

_____

_____

Death from Overdose

Drugs have their place when used properly but can bring about a disastrous outcome if obtained illegally or mis-prescribed. The result can be an addiction to the drugs or an overdose from taking the pills or taking them in excess. Drug addiction affects not only the patient but also their friends, family, and associates.

> When someone is addicted to drugs or alcohol, those who love them will hear so many different and completely contradictory schools of thought on the best ways to help them. You will hear that you have to show your support and let the addict know you are there. You will also hear that you can't enable the person, that you should completely shut them out, so they hit rock bottom. While one expert insists that you must visit and keep in touch with them while in rehab to show your encouragement, others will say to let them focus solely on their recovery without interference. When the medical professionals themselves are at odds about how to treat patients, how does a parent, sibling, friend, associate, etc. have a chance of trying to setup a plan to curb or eliminate their use of such drugs. The fact remains that no one knows the correct course of action to take when a loved one is addicted to drugs, but everyone wants to give an answer. As a result, family members and close friends are often left feeling like they are to blame after a loved one's overdose regardless of what actions they took or didn't take while the person was still alive. [56]

Opioid addiction is at an all-time high, many times resulting from a physician-issued pain regimen. Physicians are only now beginning to understand the impact of opioid use and addiction. Unfortunately, the use of opioids for pain management results in an addictive state that individuals cannot overcome. The overdose may result from a combination of alternate drug choices or an excessive dose of the prescribed drug.

Many times, the individual loved one does not mean to overdose and loses the drug battle with their life. For the survivors, it is overwhelming. Could they have done something more to monitor their use, to get them help, and rehabilitation? What might have prevented the overdose? As a family member, friend, or medical professional wonder, it is not your fault. Guilty feelings can impact the grief process further as they wonder how they might have prevented this outcome for their loved one.

They mattered; it was not your battle to control. You matter, it is your battle to come to terms with their loss and your right to continue to live. Seek a support system to aid you on your grief journey.

Roadmap to Self Help and Discovery Key Takeaways:
- ❖ Opioid addiction is at an all-time high, often resulting from a physician-issued pain regimen.
- ❖ Many times, the individual loved one does not mean to overdose and loses the drug battle with their life. For the survivors, it is overwhelming.
- ❖ They mattered; it was not your battle to control. You matter. It is your battle to come to terms with their loss and your right to continue to live. Seek a support system to aid you.

Express your emotions:
What do you know of the opioid crisis? Try to understand it was not the objective of your loved one to lose their life but to get relief from their pain and addiction. Talk to your loved ones, review your use and theirs and get professional help where possible.

_____

_____

_____

What is your action plan?

_____

_____

_____

THIRTEEN
SPIRITUAL ASSESSMENT

F inding solace and peace of mind in your religious or spiritual beliefs can be comforting, or the circumstances of your loss can rock your foundational beliefs. It takes on different approaches and importance to different people, look closely at your beliefs prior and after and try to find a way to find comfort in your loved one's situation and your own.

Religious or spiritual beliefs may also help by lending larger meaning to a loved one's life and death. or some, the belief that a loved one is enjoying the spiritual riches of heaven. Believing your loved one helps guide you in this world or that you will be reunited in another place after your own death can help you continue to feel connected with the person. If prayer heartens or sustains you, set aside time for it. Read spiritual texts that you find comforting, attend services and share your circumstances. Gardening or communing with nature, which offers ample opportunity to observe the rhythms of life and death in the natural world, is also soothing. [57]

We were fortunate enough that Susie was able to receive last rites from our uncle, Father Richard. As we gathered around saying our goodbyes and thank you, he was able to pray with us and send her on her next journey to see the Lord with peace. Susie had received blessings in the past and would have approved if she was conscious. She believed in the afterlife and that we would all reunite with our loved ones. This simple act provided me and our family comfort, along with the knowledge that we will be reunited again someday.

As a family and with friends, we created a beautiful garden in our home with her favorite flowers, colors, statues, and plaques to honor her. She resides with us at every family gathering, big or small, the butterflies love her spot, the cardinals and finches abound, and there are reflective spots to sit and feel her presence. Susie is never far from us in thoughts, and nature just reinforces the beauty she had while with us and in her new garden spot. It is nothing to see the grandchildren laughing and playing around it and saying, "We love you Susie."

Roadmap to Self Help and Discovery Key Takeaways:

❖ The reasons for the loss may have more significance if you believe in the religious or spiritual applications of life and life after death. Many find peace in knowing they are present in another form and will meet again.

❖ Working with nature can resonate with some as the circle of life is representative of nature, and the beauty of nature may provide some peace or solace. Find your peace.

Express your emotions:

What are your wishes? What of your loved ones? Have those discussions to ensure that you are doing what they would want and that they know your wishes. Plant or visit a garden.

_____

_____

_____

_____

_____

What is your action plan?

_____

_____

_____

BURIAL OR CREMATION?

Finding the right way to memorialize your loved one can be emotional. What you believe and what they believed can impact your decision on whether to bury them or cremate them. Some people find peace and solace in visiting their loved one's gravesite. Others have their cremated remains in urns or jewelry, or they have spread their ashes in a location that means something to the deceased.

> Cremation Resource: How to decide whether to cremate or bury (n.d.), states, As people nowadays live away from their family roots, cremation provides more flexibility in terms of memorialization as compared to the method of burying in a cemetery or graveyard. The cremated remains can be stored in a cremation urn and displayed on a shelf or mantle at home, scattered on land, scattered from the air by plane, floated on water, placed in a columbarium, buried in a burial plot (does not require a full-sized plot), or entombed in a crypt within a mausoleum. So, you can carry the cremated remains of the deceased with you if you are moving elsewhere; but this is not possible in case of burial. [58]

How we process information and feelings will enable us to be open to how our well-being is affected physically, emotionally, and spiritually. People deal with their loss in different ways. Some bury their loved ones, while others are cremated. Some like to visit the cemetery and care for the plots, whereas others never visit, it is too hard, or they do not feel their presence there. People with cremated remains may bury them in the garden, make an indoor garden or shrine area, or spread them in a special place, and others wear them in jewelry form.

Our family had Susie cremated. Many members of the family have a locket to hold her close, to feel her presence with them always. Her siblings and parents have small urns with her remains so that she is close regardless of where they live. This has been extremely comforting for us all.

Roadmap to Self Help and Discovery Key Takeaways:

❖ How we process information and feelings will enable us to be open to how our well-being is affected physically, emotionally, and spiritually.

❖ Discuss with your loved ones so you know their wishes, and they know your preferences.

❖ Remember your loved ones in the way that is best in line with their wishes and your healing.

Express your emotions:

What will bring you the most comfort? Share your desires and seek to understand other's views. Share your desires and views regarding end of life wishes, burial, and cremation.

_____

_____

_____

_____

_____

_____

What is your action plan?

_____

_____

_____

HOW DO RELATIONSHIPS MATTER?

The bonds we create with each other connects us and make us laugh, cry, hug, comfort, and share excitement, joy, sadness, and love. When our loved ones leave, we change forever. Some experience a sense of comfort when their loved ones pass on. My sister Carol witnessed my daughter Susie pass through my daughter Angela. Angela stated she felt Susie comfort her as she took her last breath. Others state that they felt a presence and knew she was gone.

> There should be recognition that there is rebirth after death. With the death of a loved one, your life is forever changed. The release of the energies that tied you can catalyze a transformation in your consciousness. Many testify to experiences of a transcendent nature characterized by a heightened consciousness and an in-pouring of love from an invisible source after the passing of a loved one. Others may experience revelations about themselves and deep insights into the meaning of life and the afterlife. These peak experiences may mark a time of spiritual emergence and self-realization, if classified as such rather than being viewed as periods of confusion. By surrendering to the process, you can awaken spiritually, reborn into a greater definition of yourself, and open a new meaningful chapter to your life. [59]

Life as we knew it has changed forever. The loss of a loved one will be felt and experienced in numerous different ways and make us cherish past memories and may rock our sense of belonging, safety and security, importance of past, present, and future, and being present in our relationships will be enhanced. We will become more aware of volunteerism and giving back in the community. We will have a greater sense of presenteeism to act and not put off until tomorrow as tomorrow is not guaranteed. Life is full of chapters, and the death of your loved one causes a rebirth for you as you develop your "new normal."

> After a loved one dies, the feeling of safety disappears. Adjusting to an important loss can be helped by developing or strengthening relationships with other people, seeing new places, and engaging in new activities. These new chapters of life are not meant to replace the loss but to serve as a support for the beginning of a new life phase. [60]

YOUR LOVED ONE DIED.
THEY WOULD NOT WANT YOU TO LIVE A LIFE WHERE YOU ARE DEAD INSIDE.
EMBRACE LIFE AND HONOR THEIR LIFE.

We are forever changed. The love we shared with our loved ones shifts to a new process of learning to live without their physical presence in our lives. How we handle this loss can be affected by how we respond and change ourselves, how we share those memories, and how we make new ones while helping others adapt. Consider looking at these suggestions to improve your life physically, emotionally, and spiritually.

LIVE LIFE TO ITS FULLEST. IT IS THE BEST WAY TO HONOR YOUR LOVED ONES. LIVE WELL.

Roadmap to Self Help and Discovery Key Takeaways:

❖ We are forever changed. The love we shared with our loved ones shifts to a new process of learning to live without their physical presence in our lives.

❖ Live life to its fullest. It is the best way to honor your loved ones. Live well. Enjoy relationships (new and old), participate in new activities, new travels, a new chapter in life. It does not replace but extends your story, always honoring your past chapter.

Express your emotions:

How do you relive and tell your past stories, your past chapters? What are your plans for the next chapter? Broaden your scope, make new relationships, get involved in new and old activities, travel to experience new places, and begin a new chapter? What would you do?

_____

_____

_____

What is your action plan?

_____

_____

_____

CREATE SPECIAL WAYS TO HONOR YOUR LOVED ONES.

How can we honor our loved ones? The following are some examples to consider, review the list and make up your own agenda of things that mean something to you and to your loved ones that will bring you a sense of peace, of being connected, and making a difference. It is important to be active, to create your new chapter in life cherishing the past, honoring the relationships, and merging them with the present as a way of creating a positive approach to future—a life full of passion and purpose honoring your loved one and yourself.

1. Plant a garden.
    a. Special plants or statuary to build your garden.
        i. Get others involved. They will feel part of the healing by honoring them.
        ii. Kids love to garden and enjoy being a positive part of the experience.
    b. Spend time talking to your loved ones in the garden, find your special place.
    c. Know your loved ones are represented at family functions as they're part of the garden and thus with you in spirit.

2. Memorial celebrations
    a. Give special members of the family or friends gifts instead of your loved ones on their birthday or celebration day.
    b. Make a memory book for others to write and share memories.

    c. Create note cards and attach them to balloons—release singing songs of love.

        i. Notes tell who, where, story, and email (if others find the message and want to respond).

3. Create a non-profit, scholarship in their honor, become a benefactor, make a donation to causes your loved ones supported.

4. Enjoy memorial blankets, paintings, artwork that memorialize your loved one.

5. Do something for others in their honor.

6. Donate financially or with your time to charities they supported.

    a. Whatever makes sense to your family.

    b. Make duffel bags for foster kids.

    c. Create care packages for homeless, veterans, women's shelters.

    d. Collect and wrap coloring books, crayons for kids in the hospital.

7. Attend a charity event, donate time, or walk for the cause.

8. Give back working in a soup kitchen or at a food pantry.

9. Consider something larger, such as forming a non-profit, donating a portion of your business profits to a specific charity, cultivating awareness for specific causes.

10. Talk about life and death wishes with loved ones.

11. Encourage the creation of Power of Attorney (POA).

    a. What are their expectations and desires?

    b. Do they have a trust? If not—consider creating one.

    c. Do they want to be an organ donor?

12. Difficult decisions are made easier if wishes are known.

    a. What do they want for life support choices?

    b. Upon their death:

        i. Where are their important papers?

        ii. Are your accounts and affairs in order? Assemble them and let your loved ones know where to find them.

        iii. Talk about preplanning for their death, prepayment options.

13. Talk to your minister, priest, pastor, or whomever can pray with you and guide/counsel you.

14. Pray often for yourself, your family and friends, and for your loved ones in heaven.

15. Just when you think you have done all you can,

    a. God will send help, trust and believe you are never alone.

Know when something is born (like seeds planted), something grows (greenery blooms), dreams occur (flowers bloom), death occurs (some die annually), some are perennial (they continue to grow every year). Honor and talk about your loved ones to watch them rebloom as a perennial—never totally gone—inspiring rebirth, inspiration, and salvation that life continues.

In order to help others as our Susie did, a couple friends started a jewelry business in her honor, with a portion of the proceeds going to charity.

Her family started the non-profit Susie Q's Kids in her honor to brighten and inspire the lives of children and young adults by supplying comfort bags to other non-profits: "One Bag at a Time." https://susieqskids.org/

Here is a sample of the bag contents:

How can you and your family and friends make a difference? (See Appendix D).

Roadmap to Self Help and Discovery Key Takeaways:
- ❖ Create ways to honor and give back.
- ❖ Make a difference in the lives of others and your own.

Express your emotions:
What suggestions to improve your life physically, emotionally, and spiritually resonated with you? What others can you think of that might be beneficial to you? Make your list with a timeline and plan of action. It may take time but will aid you on your healing journey.

_____

_____

_____

_____

_____

_____

_____

_____

What is your action plan?

_____

_____

_____

FOURTEEN
HELP OTHERS PREPARE FOR THE FUTURE

L earning to live without your loved one is a life-long challenge. You will be overwhelmed with memories of past times, good and bad, by current events, and regret for future events and activities that they will be unable to share and experience. You may be having a good day and someone else may experience a loss, an illness, or special event that will affect you. Being aware of your responses will enable you to address them and refrain from entering the depression rabbit hole or, in some cases, thoughts of suicide as the only avenue.

Reach out to your support team: your doctor, therapist, group support members, your family, work associates, and friends. Express your feelings to them. They cannot fix you or your feelings, but they can let you know you are not alone. By sharing your feelings, you may be able to share a story, a tear, a laugh, and find that balance of acceptance.

As a family member, friend or associate, you must also be aware of what others are feeling, saying or not saying. There are coping mechanisms that must be watched, as suicide can affect you or anyone. The person may be retreating from everyone, talking irrationally, talking of suicide, or simply seem too upbeat for the situation.

Suicide has impacted our family. We have family and friends who had challenges or suffered from PSTD, including Uncle Keith who suffered from PSTD after several tours in the Army. He lost his way and ended his life, leaving their family and friends with a huge loss and unbearable sadness and guilt. We were left wondering what we might have done to aid him, and for all the lost future conversations and events.

WHAT IS SUICIDE?

Suicide results in the death of an individual, but it really impacts everyone they know from close family and friends to acquaintances and associates. Their loss could involve harming others depending on their method and approach to ending their own lives. Suicide is the outcome of mental illness. We need to understand how depression, anxiety, stress, and insecurity may impact our ability to see the world in a positive way and ask for help when needed.

According to the National Institute of Mental Health, Suicide is when people direct violence at themselves with the intent to end their lives, and they die because of their actions. Additionally, the effects of suicide go beyond the person who acts to take his or her life: it can have a lasting effect on family, friends, and communities. The National Institute of Mental Health (NIMH) website has resources that can help you, a friend, or a family member learn about the signs and symptoms, risk factors and warning signs, and ongoing research about suicide and suicide prevention.[61]

Numerous local and national organizations address suicide prevention awareness as well as counseling and therapy centers that are willing to discuss your personal situation, fears, anxieties, and help you develop a plan of action for well-being. Seek support.

Roadmap to Self Help and Discovery Key Takeaways:

❖ Reach out to your support team: your doctor, therapist, group support members, your family, work associates, and friends. Express your feelings to them. They cannot fix you or your feelings, but they can let you know you are not alone. By sharing your feelings, you may be able to share a story, a tear, a laugh, and find that balance of acceptance.

❖ Numerous local and national organizations address suicide prevention awareness as well as counseling and therapy centers that are willing to discuss your situation, fears, anxieties, and help you develop a plan of action for well-being.

❖ Seek support.

Express your emotions:

What is your support system comprised of? What do you understand about suicide awareness? Educate yourself so you can help yourself or someone else. Get involved, participate in a walk.

_____

_____

What is your action plan?

_____

_____

How Can You Help

Learn more about suicide—do your homework. By being educated, you may be able to recognize symptoms in yourself or in others and be able to offer suggestions or contact information to address it. Many times, those thinking suicidal thoughts don't feel they have any other alternatives. They cannot talk about this taboo subject and thus dwell on it themselves and many times make it worse.

With your education and awareness, talk freely of it to others so they know you might be a safe person to broach the subject with. Awareness is key! Listen to yourself and your friends, watch email and text messages for potential triggers, and watch their Facebook posts and social media accounts for alarming comments. Make that phone call, send an email or text, or send a Messenger note to let them know they are not alone. Just show up even when they say it's not necessary. Sometimes that blueness is so enveloping that we push others away when in reality they could change the focus of the day to something more positive. Think about it, try to make them laugh or think of a way to overcome the issue of their insecurity.

Talk about using your doctor or therapist as a resource, how they have helped you through your own life challenges. Encourage yourself and others to seek guidance where professionals can help work through life's trials, hiccups, and insecurities. They can help you with medication at times, counseling, self-help activities, and group therapy. I have used all of these and encourage others dealing with life's struggles to do the same. An impartial third party trained in the ways to help that is the best option.

Attend suicide prevention awareness events. My family and I support the American Foundation for Suicide Prevention (AFSP) by attending events and walking in support of awareness, support for those dealing with the loss of loved ones and for those struggling with the decision. Walking with them and speaking of our lost ones, mentioning names, and asking for their stories offers support. Mention their loved one's names, and offering our condolences makes it easier to deal with the unrealistic aspects of suicide.

As a Tragedy Assistance Program for Survivors (TAPS) peer mentor, I assist military families that are grieving the loss of a member of the armed forces. By listening and supporting others, we make a difference, sometimes between life and death.

Roadmap to Self Help and Discovery Key Takeaways:
- ❖ Many times, those thinking suicidal thoughts don't feel they have any other alternatives.
- ❖ With your education and awareness, talk freely of it to others so they know you might be a safe person. Knowledge is key.
- ❖ Listen to yourself and your friends, you may have the ability to change the outcome.

Express your emotions:
Be present in the moment. Take the time to listen to others and share your emotions. Be willing to open up and live in the moment offering or receiving support when needed.

_____

_____

_____

_____

_____

_____

What is your action plan?

_____

_____

_____

SUICIDE PREVENTION AWARENESS AND COPING CONTACTS

Review Appendix D for a list of resources.

❖ Contact information for you or someone you know who may be in crisis can be found on the National Institute of Mental Health website: https://www.nimh.nih.gov/health/publications/suicide-faq/index.shtml.

❖ Call the toll-free National Suicide Prevention Lifeline (NSPL) at 1–800–273–TALK (8255), 24 hours a day, 7 days a week. The service is available to everyone.

❖ The deaf and hard of hearing can contact the Lifeline via TTY at 1–800–799–4889.

❖ Contact social media outlets directly if you are concerned about a friend's social media updates or dial 911 in an emergency.

❖ Learn more on the National Suicide Prevention Lifeline (NSPL) website.

❖ The Crisis Text Line is another resource, available 24 hours a day, 7 days a week. Text "home" to 741741.

FIFTEEN
SO COMFORTED BY A RECENT VISITATION

My girl Susie McBride-Welsh has been gone for close to two years. I was exhausted emotionally from our grieving meeting the night before as another family's story hit very close to home. I took my elderly mom (going on 92) and who lives with us, for another doctor appointment and test early one Friday morning, a normal occurrence. We got home, and I fell asleep in the chair.

I don't usually like to sleep as I am always trying to find Susie and wake crying because I can never find her. My dream starts with my mom in a doctor's office. Of course, my mom is hitting on the doctor; the doctor says she needs surgery (she doesn't, it's a dream); the nurse says we will have a bunch of pre-op appointments, then surgery, rehab facility, and home physical therapy. Can I say it is tiring just to think of it?

I leaned over my mom to comfort her, and suddenly she changed into my daughter Susie. She sat up and gave me the biggest damned hug, I can still feel it. I just hung on and cried, "I miss you so much, I love you." She said, "It's going to be OK mom, I am always with you, love you mom."

As I reiterated my plea, she said again, "It's OK mom, I love you, I am always with you mom," and she was gone.

Reflecting on the second anniversary of her death, I had been thinking a lot about Susie and had started the non-profit Susie Q's Kids (officially approved as a 501c3 by the government), was talking to everyone about it, had finished the draft of my grieving book, and was working on two children's book along with caring for my elderly mom.

- *Susie Q's Kids Positive Reflections: My Special Angel* addresses the questions a child may pose after the loss of a loved one.

- *Susie Q's Kids Positive Reflections: Good Characteristics* is a coloring book that reflects on the positive aspects a child should model.

I so needed that hug and those words. I know I found my purpose with the nonprofit and writing, but it provided me peace. Truly thankful and blessed, I hope this story gives you some sense of comfort. Susie came in my dreams when I least expected it. I finally feel she is OK, and she knows we are too. She said she is always with us. Please take some comfort from my experience. My nightmares have ceased. I hope you find some solace from my words.

I wish the same for you!

Roadmap to Self Help and Discovery Key Takeaways:
- ❖ Be open to signs and interpreting them.
- ❖ Embrace the moments, the interpretation, and share with others who may be missing them or someone else.
- ❖ Enjoy the moment.

Express your emotions:

Have you experienced a visitation? Do you see butterflies, cardinals, pennies, dimes, or other items that make you think of your loved ones? (I love sunflowers and butterflies) Ask others to share their sightings or experiences.

_____

_____

_____

_____

_____

_____

_____

What is your action plan?

_____

_____

_____

SIXTEEN
CONCLUSION

Many books have sad chapters or elements, take control and write your next chapter in life with passion and purpose.

When life forces your hand, embrace the new chapter. Every new beginning comes from some other beginning's end. [62]

Every day we are present in a chapter of our lives and impacted by those previous chapters. Just like a book, some chapters are building blocks for others. Some are suspenseful, whereas others are ordinary day-to-day life, some are sad, some are happy, how you choose to live your chapters is up to you. Embrace each chapter with a belief that you are making the best of each day. Choose wisely.

Early chapters

We started as babies, learning about everything from the family and friends who surrounded us. As we grew, we learned new things and had new experiences daily. We met the kids on the block, children of our parents' friends, kids at daycare, and on the playground. We learned to climb the play structures, ride the swing, and go up and down the slide.

We learned to ride a baby scooter, a tricycle, a bike with training wheels, a regular bike, a motorcycle, or a car. We learned to tread water, doggie paddle, and swim, overcoming fears of the water.

We started daycare, kindergarten, first grade, middle school, high school, and university, adjusting to the anxiety of each passing grade, the new faces, the new trials, the new teachers, and the new expectations of each grade.

We learned to socialize and make friends and sometimes enemies as we moved in and out of relationships (some good, some not so good). We attended gatherings, went on dates, dances, proms, and found some friendships were fleeting and others traveled the passage of time as lifelong friendships evolved.

We moved to new homes and new jobs, leaving those we knew and were comfortable with and meeting new people in new places and having new experiences.

We got involved in the arts or sports, participating and listening. We attended concerts, musicals, plays, and sporting games. We clapped, sang, yelled, laughed, and cried as we related to the different events.

We tended to our elders, our spouses, and our children. We gave birth and said goodbye. We suffered at the hand of broken relationships, friendships that ended, relationships that ended in separation or divorce, those who moved away, and those who died.

We learned a lesson with each chapter of our life. We were anxious, excited, happy, sad, healthy, sick, and just lived in the moment.

As the chapter regarding the death of our loved one started, we cried and yelled. We became frustrated, lost, and we despaired that we would ever be able to exist and be normal again. We suffered, reminisced, and learned the strength we had inside to survive.

Your new chapter starts as your new normal gets used to the change that occurred. The pain is still there but is more manageable. The love for your lost one drives you to be your best in their honor.

Welcome your new chapter with determination that your focus on life is the best tribute you can give your loved one.

Remember, Reflect, Recreate, and Relate. You are unstoppable, believe in yourself, and your passion and purpose will re-emerge. You will grow and smile again, the new you.

Your new you, your new normal protects you. It is the process necessary to travel and explore your journey after the death of your loved ones. The fog encompassing your coping protects your mind and body from the pain. Be kind to yourself, take the moments, celebrate your wins, mourn your losses, and live again. The violence of the storm will diminish, the rain will come and go, and the sun will shine again. You are not the same; shine and celebrate your new you.

You are amazing. Remember that your new normal embraces your strength and honors your loved ones.

You are stronger than you think. Live life to its fullest.

Dear loved ones,

Your presence surrounds me. It permeates my existence.

You are always with me in my heart, my mind, my soul, and my memories.

Although you are physically gone, you live on in all our thoughts and

possess a part of our daily lives.

Thumbs Up, we love you.

Good luck on your journey.
Stay positive, your loved ones are always with you!

EPILOGUE

The grief journey is ongoing, the future is still unfolding. As I move through the future chapters and continue traveling the path of my Journey into the Looking Glass, Susie will remain loved, missed, and cherished. We will overcome future obstacles with passion and purpose as we are survivors and committed to our well-being and that of others. More to come.

SYNOPSIS

Although the ache of losing a loved one cannot be escaped, it can be a catalyst for positive change. Dr. Mary described her relationship, the grief process, and how she harnessed the worst moments in her life to create a transparent book of her journey and self-help and discovery topics to aid others in their grieving process. Her strength comes from sharing her story and the hope that others find solace and inspiration on their own journeys with the passion for leading purposeful lives.

The Four Aspects of Positive Reflection: Remember * Reflect * Recreate * Relate

- ❖ Remember: Understand Your Past and How Your Loved Ones Impacted You–Remember the Good and Bad Memories

- ❖ Reflect: Understand Your Journey and Path to Grasping the Impact You Had on Your Loved Ones and They Had on You

- ❖ Recreate: Get in Touch and Come to Grips with Them– Embrace Your New Normal

❖ Relate: Make Your Commitment to Your "New Normal" Give of Yourself for a Better Life–Practice Self-care, Supporting Others, and Giving Back in the Community

Intent of the book, a Passport to Self-Discovery and Reflection:

❖ Understand the devastation of loss and learn how to cope with the stages of grief and their feelings.

❖ Reflect on the different aspects of grief and channel your thoughts on your grief journey.

❖ Realize you have a choice to wallow in despair or focus your energies positively.

❖ Weave through the grief journey and how Dr. Mary handled the challenges and the inexplainable pain.

❖ Utilize the key takeaways and self-help and discovery sections to learn how to handle the different aspects knowing you do not travel alone on your grief journey.

❖ Find comfort, inspiration, and purpose moving forward with your life.

ABOUT THE AUTHOR

Dr. Welsh co-founded the non-profit Susie Q's Kids following the death of her daughter, Susie McBride-Welsh. Susie Q's Kids raises awareness for other non-profits which distributes their comfort bags "One Bag at a Time" brightening and inspiring the lives of children and young adults.

As an Author, Speaker, and Grief Session Facilitator, she documented the first two years of her journey for people who have suffered the loss of a child or loved one or supporting those that are experiencing such a loss. Her goal is to support their grief journey with information and provide a program to guide them on their journey.

She also acts as a Tragedy Assistance Program for Survivors (TAPS) Peer Mentor for fallen military survivors providing guidance, support, and companionship to those in the grieving process.

As a Grief Session Facilitator, Entrepreneur, University Professor, Business Strategist, HR Talent Executive, and Chief People Person, she has a passion and purpose for helping others. Through her writing, mentoring, courses, and speaking engagements, she hopes to instill a framework for grievers to find comfort in their new circumstances and a life of passion and purpose.

Dr. Mary is happily married to Joseph Welsh with six amazing children and five awesome grandchildren that fill her life with happiness as well as being surrounded by her cherished mother, mother-in-law, father-in-law, and a tribe of loving family and friends.

APPENDIX A
POEMS THAT SPEAK
FROM THE HEART

Through the use of poetry, sentiment and feelings can be shared and felt. I hope you find solace in these poems to aid you on your self-discovery journey.

Please enjoy these poems from my perspective that speak from the heart.

WHEN IT WAS YOUR TIME TO LEAVE US

When it was your time to leave us
We gathered around and
shared special moments.
We gave one last hug and kiss.
We sang "You Are My Sunshine."
We graced your journey with prayer.
We said goodbye with heavy hearts.

Your presence was with us one moment
and gone the next, leaving a huge void.
We wanted to pull you back but

you had taken your last labored breath and
you were finally at peace.

We must learn to live without
your contagious smile;
attempt to live as you did in life:
kind and caring, making a difference in
the lives of others.

Our "new normal" without you
feels so lonely at times.
Then it feels no different,
like you are still with us.
Your presence permeates our lives.

The memories, the pictures, the music,
the jewelry, and the garden.
The dreams, the pennies, the butterflies,
the dandelions, and the cardinals:
We simply have to be receptive to feel
your love enveloping us.

Thank you for gracing our lives
here on earth and
continuing our journey with us
here on earth.

We look forward to our next journey
where we will unite.

"You Got This," and "We Got This."
Until we meet again, Shine on Sunshine.

DR. MARY WELSH

YOU ARE OUR RAY OF SUNSHINE

You are our Sunshine.
You made everyone feel special.
Your smile radiated.
Your hugs embraced easily.
Your love was given freely.

How do we live without you?
Simply by remembering you and
your presence.
We share our precious memories.

We speak of you often and freely
without reluctance.
We take care of those you
loved and cherished.
We do good deeds in your honor.

We remember and rejoice that
you are pain free.
We relish the fact that we will meet again
forever loved, our Ray of Sunshine.

WHAT'S IT LIKE IN HEAVEN?

What's it like in heaven?
Are you hanging with our family and
friends that arrived before you?
Did you tell them how much we missed them,
give them hugs for us?

Are the angels as beautiful as we thought?
Did they welcome you with open arms?
Do they embrace you even now in our absence?
Do you get to sing, dance, and fly free-spirited?

It makes me smile to see the clouds and
think of you.
To see the brilliance of the sun and
think of you.
To witness the flurry of a storm and
think of you.
It doesn't take much to think of you.

Life is different without you.
I want to share new moments,
new stories, new dreams.

And then I remember you are not physically here.
But you are, in every sunshiny day,
every cloudy day, and every storm.

You are wound in the fabric of our lives and
thus, forever with us, today and every day.
Shine on, Sunshine.

You Are Missed

You are missed.
You are loved.
We wish it was all a bad dream.
We want to wake up and
have you here with us.

The days are long without you.
The nights are even longer.
Some days, it is hard to get up and get motivated.
Other days, we embrace the day remembering you.

The memories keep us going.
Talking about you energizes us,
you are not forgotten.

Doing good in your honor is rewarding.
Thanks for being you and showing us
how to live fully.
"You Got This," and "We Got This."

WHEN SOMEONE YOU LOVE BECOMES A MEMORY,
THE MEMORY IS TREASURED.

SOME PEOPLE ARE GOOD, SOME ARE EXTRA-SPECIAL

Some people are good,
some are extra-special.
You are that extra-special,
a beacon of light in the darkness.

You have always reached out with
a phone call, a card, or a visit.
You took up collections for those in need.

You shared your time with others to
teach, mentor, and support them.
You provided love and support to
those hurt and suffering.
You made others feel loved and important.
Your smile made others smile.

Your memories and good deeds live on.
Your family and friends continue to
live like you did.
They are binding together to create opportunities
to remember you and to honor
your shared experiences helping others.

We formed a non-profit to
continue your good works.
Susie Q's Kids, providing comfort to children
"One Bag at a Time."
We will bring joy and support to
others in your honor.

You are wound in the fabric of
our lives and thus forever with us,
today and every day.
Shine on, Sunshine.

Happiness springs from doing good and
helping others. [63]
Make a difference!

WE ARE SORRY

We are sorry.
You should not have experienced pain.
You should have been pain-free.
It was not your lot in life.

We are sorry.
For all the days and nights in the hospital,
All the doctor visits and tests.

We are sorry.
But so proud of the way you handled it.
You lived life fully, cherished life, and
those you loved.

We are sorry.
You missed events and gatherings
due to your illness.
We wish you had gotten to enjoy life more.

We are sorry.
When the end arrived that
we could not save you.
We honored your wishes to
withhold life support.

We are sorry.
We wanted to hold you longer,
to love you more.
But we promised and let you go
until we meet again.
Shine on, Sunshine

LIFE IS FULL OF SEASONS

Life is full of seasons.
The way we celebrate them involves
those we love.
Each season makes us remember you.
Smile, laugh, and cherish wonderful moments.

Our garden blossoms with the beauty of the
flowers, trees, and shrubs.
The sculptures of good times and memories.
You are present during every family gathering,
day at the pool, or quiet moment.

Winter snow and ice, snow angels, toboggan rides,
snow forts, and snow fights.
Laughter with cold breaths
enjoying a wintry day.

Spring rains and flowers blossom
Singing in the rain,
watching the daffodils and tulips bloom.
Watching the butterflies and
listening to the birds sing.

Summer sunshine and warmth comfort us.
Days by the pool,
gathering together to laugh and have fun.
Taking kids for bike rides, wagon rides, and
taking long strolls.
Going camping, family gatherings, fireworks,
beaches, and parks.

Fall cool weather and hoodies,
Watching the flowers and trees change colors.
Sitting around a campfire, s'mores,
marshmallows, and friends.
Going to the cider mill, pumpkins, and
trick-or-treating.

Regardless of the season
You are always with us, we remember you,
we share stories, and we celebrate you.

Thanks for being our Ray of Sunshine, Shine On.

FAMILY AND LOSS

Mom and daughter
Daughters are the best friends
a mom could have.
They are full of the passion of life and
love sharing it with you.

Moms losing a daughter feel lost,
their lifetime buddy is missing.
All the hopes, dreams, and future
aspirations are gone.

Dad and daughter
Daughters are the pride of their dads.
They are the miniature princesses
he loves to cherish.

Dads losing a daughter feel loss at not being able
to prevent their pain and loss.
All the hopes, dreams, and
future aspirations are gone.

Sisters
Sisters are bound by a special bond that
knows no bounds.
They share laughter, tears,
happiness, sadness, and dreams.

The loss of a sister challenges
their own being, their own dreams.
All the hopes, dreams, and
future aspirations are gone.

Brothers and Sisters
their whole life.

Been their hero, been their friend,
been their confidante, and protector.
Their loss leaves a life-long void.
All the hopes, dreams, and
future aspirations are gone.

Aunts, nieces, and nephews
Aunts want to protect and love
their nieces and nephews.
They want to have that special connection and
be the "favorite auntie."

The loss of being in their lives as they grow is
almost unbearable.
All the hopes, dreams, and
future aspirations are gone.

Family
Grandparents, aunts, uncles, and cousins.
They have shared life relationships,
strong ties, and bonds.

The loss of a granddaughter, niece, or a cousin
impacts who they are.
Their loss is unimaginable,
how will the future play out without them?
All the hopes, dreams, and
future aspirations are gone.

Friends
Friends share the experiences of life.
They share the firsts, the happiest,
the silliest, and the saddest.
They are a constant, they are there.

The loss of a good friend can be overwhelming or
a catalyst for change.
All the hopes, dreams, and
future aspirations are gone.

Family and Friends
How will we continue to live without you?
How can we grasp the loss of
future hopes, dreams, and future aspirations?

Be with us, send us signs, and
embrace us with your love from afar.

Be there to support us here on earth and
when we start our next journey with you.

YOU ARE IN CONTROL—FIND YOUR PURPOSE

You are in control
You are responsible for your destiny.
We cannot prevent death, but
We can control how we respond.
We can let it define us or we can define it.

Respect yourself.
Respect those you love.
Respect those gone that you loved.
Honor them by living a full life.

Take charge.
Get up, get moving, and get motivated.
Find your new purpose.

Dedicate yourself to supporting
your purpose.
Enjoy life, create your own ray of sunshine.
Shine on in their honor.

"What is your purpose?"

WHAT WOULD THEY WANT?

What would they want?
We can get lost in the past or
We can live the life they would want for us.

When overwhelmed with the tangible loss,
Appreciate those signs they send you.
They are always with you.

When you rally against the injustice of your loss,
When you long to hold and cuddle them,
Remember their face, their smile, and
the twinkle in their eyes.
Hug a comfort item that reminds
you of them:
They are always with you.

When you find yourself wanting to
share a moment with them,
When you long to speak to them,
Do it in any form you can.
Talk to them, write, journal, and share.
They listen, they are always with you.

Live life to the best of your ability.
Your loved ones would want this.
They would not want you to wallow in
darkness, pain, and sorrow.

Remember them fondly and
smile the way they remember you.

Celebrate the life you shared and
live now for you both as they
are always with you.

For those who love with all their
heart and soul,
There are no goodbyes as
we are always connected.

FROM DAD'S PERSPECTIVE

Parents of child loss will say that their
grief will always be with them.
Others say that "forever" is too long to grieve and
they try to fix the grieving parent.

The problem is a broken heart can
never be fixed.
Losing a child is to lose part of your soul.
How can that be fixed? It can't.

Losing a child is to lose a huge part of the future and
a million dreams.
How can that be fixed? It can't.
Losing a child is to have
one's heart shattered.
How can that be fixed? It can't.

The grief from child loss is a forever grief.
Yes, we will eventually find a place in grief that is less raw.
Yes, we will be able to manage grief more as
we continue on this journey of loss.

Yes, we will be able to see the sun
shine once again,
but it will never shine the same.
..
Losing a child is the most difficult pain
known to humankind and the grief lasts forever.

There is no "fix" for a heart that has been
broken by child loss.
We work hard every day to learn how to
live within this brokenness.
Dad shared (unknown author).[64]

"The journey of surviving a child loss
is indescribable.

When you died,
the hardest thing was realizing
that I had to live my life without you."[65]

THE CHRISTMAS HOLIDAYS ARRIVE WITHOUT YOU

The Christmas holidays arrive without you.
I find myself thinking more of you,
the memories and the what-ifs,
The thought of you never being
physically with us hurts.
The mind knows you have no pain, but wonders
if you can feel mine and others.

The loss takes me down the
rabbit hole of depression,
wanting the holidays to simply be over.
The next minute I want to share memories of
the fun times we had and
revel in the love we shared.

Others try to understand,
but how can they when
I don't really understand
my emotional rollercoaster?
One minute I am crying,
the next planning the day without you
so that we have some normalcy.

Your loss is felt everywhere, in my waking and
in my sleeping hours.
Your presence is with us in the form of
shared songs, memories,
pictures, ornaments, and traditions.

Your presence is felt in the form of
heavenly pennies or dimes,
Facebook memories, and angels.

We create ornaments, bake cookies,
wear our pajamas, and
spoil the kids like we did together.

We continue to get new outfits,
get our hair done, and share
days at the nail salon,
always thinking of you.

We buy presents for others in your honor to
keep your name and memories alive.

The tree is adorned with new ornaments;
many angels grace our decorations.

All in all, the day arrives and
disappears without you.
Life continues and it seems so unfair.

The year comes to a close and the finality of
your loss is so unreal and hard to accept.

My search for why, the rationale of why it
was you and not me, haunts me.

In reflection, surrounded by those you love and
basking in your love and presence,
my purpose on this earth is crystal clear.

Thanks for bringing me clarity.
We will continue to live and love each other,
to support each other.

We will share your story, the impact your life had
on your family, your friends, and others.

We will aid others less fortunate in your honor
with good deeds and acts of kindness,
thus, continuing to remember the valued life and
contributions you made.

So Merry Christmas, Sunshine.
Shine over us with your brilliance.
You are so loved,
so cherished, and so missed.

FAMILY—WHERE LIFE BEGINS AND NEVER ENDS.

APPENDIX B
DEDICATION POEMS FROM SUSIE Q

Susie Q and I were very close. We talked many a day and night about those in our family, friends, work, and life in general. I took the liberty to write these poems on her behalf to demonstrate her love of life, her love for her family and friends, and how much she loved and appreciated those in her life. Please accept these poems on her behalf and mine as tributes to her loved ones and to those grieving the loss of a loved one. Perhaps the sentiment in these poems will resonate with you.

Susie McBride-Welsh

Lovingly Susie Q

MOM

Dear Mom,
If you could witness my peace,
you would embrace yourself with peace that
you were the "best mom."

If you felt my overwhelming sense of release from
my pain, you would rejoice.

If you knew how much I loved you and
was with you always,
you would stop crying and smile.

If you saw the beauty of life in my smile,
you would radiate the world with yours as
"you are amazing."

If you appreciated my good deeds on earth,
You would honor me by helping others,
making a difference.

If you want to remember me with love, then
live life to its fullest,
continue to love unconditionally and
know that I am always with you and
will comfort and guide you on your journey
until we meet again.

If the sunshine reminds you of my thirst for life,
then shine on, mommy.

I love you to the moon and back.
"I love my momma."

Susie McBride is with **Mary Welsh**.
September 9, 2016 · 🌐   · · ·

Momma,

I don't know what I'd do without you. Please know that I see and know how hard you work and how you do everything for me. I know it takes a major toll on you physically, mentally, and emotionally coming to the hospital and sitting with me everyday and making sure I am feeling ok and that I have everything I need yet you are still by my side everyday. I don't know how you do it. Thank you for everything. You are superwoman for real. Words can't express how I truly feel about you. Thank you for everything. I love you so much!!!!

❤️ Love   💬 Comment

DAD—JOE WELSH

Dear Dad,
If you knew how much you meant to me,
your heart would be bursting with pride.

If you understood why
I asked you to adopt me,
you understand the depth of my love.

If you could see my love through my eyes,
you would see my respect, love, and
honor at your sacrifices and how you loved
my mom, me, and the rest of our family.

If you could witness my release from pain,
you would holler with joy, as
it feels so good, dad.

If you saw my pride in what you do and
how I respected you,
you will continue to help others and honor me
by doing so. Thanks, daddy.

If you knew I laughed along with you,
you could hear my belly laughs now
—please continue to enjoy life.

If you saw my tears as I watch
how you treat my mom,
know you are the richest man in the world.
Thanks, dad for loving her; hold her tight and
console each other.

Just remember my love, and that
I am with you always.

If the sunshine reminds you of my
thirst for life, then shine on, daddy.

I love you to the moon and back.

Lovingly Susie Q /Dr. Mary Welsh

Those we love don't leave us,
they are with us every step of the way.
I love my papa.

MY BIG BRO

Dear Jim,
If you knew how much I admired you,
you would stand even taller.

If you understood the impact you had on me,
you would burst with love and pride.

If you could see my love for you
from my eyes,
I fear you would explode from the
sense of my love.

If you remember all our goofy,
happy, and sad times,
you would know you are my hero and
I love you.

If you saw my pride in your efforts as a
partner and dad, your heart would swell from
my pride, my love for you all, and know
I will be there for each of you
on your journeys.

If you understand gratitude,
you know my heart beats because of you,
my best friend and hero.

If you want to continue to honor me,
be the best you can and
take care of all the family,
especially our sister Angie.

If the sunshine reminds you of
my thirst for life, then shine on bro.
You are my Hero.

I love you to the moon and back.

Lovingly Susie Q /Dr Mary Welsh

MY BIG SIS

Dear Angie,
If you could visit me,
you would never be sad again.

If you understood my pain was gone and
I have so much peace, you would rejoice.

If you knew how much I appreciated
your efforts to comfort me,
you would find peace in my angel arms
wrapped around you always.

If you saw my pride in knowing how much
you loved me, our bro, and our family,
you will wrap them a little tighter
in your arms for me,
love them a little harder, and
know I am with you always,
so proud of you.

If you could see my life through my eyes,
you would see a lifetime of
"peace, love, and spandex,"
a life full of good memories and an overwhelming
sense of being loved and
loving you and others.

If you could make my life even better,
you will continue to help others
honoring me and making a difference like
you made in my life.

If you understand gratitude,
you know my dark days were
brighter and my happiest days were sweeter
because of you, my best friend,
my confidante, and protector.

Be the best you can and take care of all the family,
especially our brother Jim.

If the sunshine reminds you of my thirst for life,
then shine on sis.

I love you because you are
awesome just like me.
Big sisters rock!

I love you to the moon and back.

Lovingly Susie Q /Dr. Mary Welsh

MY SIBLINGS

Dear Brothers and Sisters,
Whether related biologically, by marriage, or
by my own definition,
I was truly blessed with
all of you as my siblings.

If you understood how loved I felt,
you would know that I was and
always will be with you.
During times of happiness, sorrow, or
silence, I am there.

At those important events and those
quiet moments, I am there.

Remember me fondly,
if you knew the depth of my love and caring,
your tears would disappear, and
your smile would radiate.

If you need me,
just look at the beauty around you,
I dance around the sun,
the moon, and the stars,
I frolic in the flower gardens,
walk on the beach,
I sing and act silly always,
but lastly listen to my laughter
on the wind that brushes your face,
I am always near.

If the sunshine reminds you of
my thirst for life, then shine on forever.

I love you to the moon and back.

Lovingly Susie Q /Dr. Mary Welsh

My Grandparents

Dear Grandparents,
If you could see me now,
you would stop crying and
know that I am better than fine.

If you knew how much I loved you,
you would smile and laugh again like
I remember you.

If you understood the depth of love,
respect, and pride I got from you,
you would stand taller, smile brighter, and
feel an overwhelming sense of my love.

If you saw and felt my pride in
being your granddaughter,
you would remember the times we shared,
the hopes and dreams we shared, and
the overwhelming love I felt and
continue to wrap around you.

If you knew how much I like to help others,
you would know
I learned how to live with
my heart on my sleeve from you,
always giving and helping others,
demonstrating respect and love
in all my actions.

If you want to honor me,
honor me by helping others, and especially
by taking care of my mom and dad.

If the sunshine reminds you of
my thirst for life, then shine on forever.

I love you to the moon and back.

Lovingly Susie Q /Dr. Mary Welsh

DR. MARY WELSH

MY LOVING NIECES AND NEPHEWS

Dear Loved Ones,
If you could see me,
you would know I am an angel
watching over you and
supporting you always.

If you feel my presence,
it is because I am wrapping
my arms around you,
clapping at your accomplishments,
brushing away your tears,
laughing at your antics, and
loving you always.

If you have a good day or a bad day,
talk to me--I will always be there
to listen, joyful or offering a hug
to make you feel better.

If you remain open,
I will send you signs of my presence:
a penny from heaven,
a dandelion puff drifting by,
a beautiful butterfly,
a cardinal watching you, or
I may arrive in your dreams
—be receptive as I am reaching out
to let you know you are never alone.

If you want to honor me,
honor me by helping your parents,
your family, your friends, and others.

If you wonder how much I love you,
look inside yourself and
you will know my love
beats within your heart.

If the sunshine reminds you of
my thirst for life, then shine on forever.

I love you to the moon and back.

Lovingly Susie Q /Dr. Mary Welsh

My Family and Friends

Dear Family and Friends,
Where to begin? You might be a sibling,
an aunt or uncle, a cousin, or
an adopted family member by
family relationship or friendship.
You might be my friend, associate, or
close to someone I know.

If you could see me now, you would see
a happy, pain-free spirit.

If you felt that spirit touch or
sense of presence,
you know I am with you always.

If you could see my life through my eyes,
you would know that I cherish the life
I led because of you all;
always loved, respected, trusted,
cherished, and never alone
—always surrounded with your presence.

If you know that I am with you always,
you will feel my joy during those
times of accomplishment,
my pride as you face all the challenges of life
—good and bad,
my arms when you are sad,
my laughter when you walk into door walls,
do goofy things, sit around the campfire,
swim in the pool, and have barbeques,

feel my love as you grow,
accomplish things, get married,
have babies, graduate, and enjoy life.

If you understand the depth of my love,
you will live, love and
find peace in this life on earth and
know I will travel with you here and
be there to welcome you
at the end of this journey.

If you want to honor me,
honor me by helping others and
especially by taking care of each other.

If the sunshine reminds you of
my thirst for life,
then shine on forever.

I love you to the moon and back.

Lovingly Susie Q /Dr. Mary Welsh

TO THOSE GRIEVING

Dear Grievers,
If you could see the world from
my perspective,
you would rejoice, as
your loved ones are at peace.

If you knew how much you are loved,
you would smile and
laugh again wrapped in the
love of your loved one.

If you understood that we
feel no pain or remorse,
you would understand we've heard all
your "what- ifs," your "if-onlys," and
other regrets, and we know the
depth of your love, your regrets,
your words unsaid,
your deeds undone, and
how much you love us.

If you love us,
know we feel your laughter, your sadness, your
accomplishments, and your pain.
We are with you every step of
your journey on earth and
await your arrival at
the end of your journey.

If you understand the depth of
our love for each other, know this:
"You Got This."

Take a deep breath,
talk to your family and friends
—lean on each other,
get professional help, and
never consider joining me
before your time is up
—never commit suicide,
as you are needed here and
others do not need to live
with the guilt of your loss and
how they may have prevented your decision.

If you understood my love of life,
help me by honoring others.

Make a difference by being a good friend,
lending an ear, providing a shoulder to lean on,
supporting others who are sick or grieving,
aiding others dealing with personal or professional
challenges, and celebrating our accomplishments.
The way you treat others is a reflection of you
being the best you can be.

"You Got This."

If the sunshine reminds you of my thirst for life,
then shine on.

I love you to the moon and back.

Loving Susie Q /Dr. Mary Welsh

LIFE IS FULL OF HAPPY MOMENTS!
REMEMBER THEM AND ME FONDLY.

CELEBRATE LIFE

These poems demonstrate how a life ends and another begins: the earthly presence ends, but the loved one continues on their new journey. For those left behind, the end of a loved one's life not only begins the mourning of their death—it is the mourning of their own life. For the life they knew is no longer valid. A new normal is unraveling along with their journey of grief and loss—of unfathomable loss.

How we deal with it is up to each of us. Our loved ones would not want us to drown in our sorrow. "You are Amazing. You Got This."

APPENDIX C

DR. MARY WELSH AND ASSOCIATED SERVICES

DR. MARY WELSH BACKGROUND

Dr. Mary Welsh has had a successful career in business leadership and helping organizations attract, train, and retain the best talent. Her non-profit leadership at Susie Q's Kids in honor of her daughter Susie McBride-Welsh is opening doors for many different non-profits to extend their missions through distribution of our comfort bags to brighten and inspire the lives of children and young adults "One Bag at a Time." This has created a platform for her to be a sought-after Speaker and Grief Session Facilitator sharing her perspectives and approach to overcoming change and living a life of happiness full of purpose. She promotes healing with her courses and speaking engagements that support sharing, understanding, and learning through an online platform in correlation with her book: *Journey into the Looking Glass: Finding Hope After the Loss of Loved Ones.*

She hopes to bring an avenue for businesses and individuals to support non-profits dedicated to aiding children and young adults, brightening and inspiring the lives of others, and making a difference "One Bag at a Time" as well as aiding families as the grieve the loss of their loved ones.

OTHER BOOKS BY THE AUTHOR

Dr. Mary Welsh, Author, National Speaker, and Grief Session Facilitator desires to aid those facing adversity and grief with a positive perspective. Consider reading her additional resources:

Journey into the Looking Glass: The Four Aspects of Positive Reflection Journal

- A journal to document your thoughts as you Remember, Reflect, Recreate, and Relate.

Susie Q's Kids Positive Reflections: My Special Angel

- A children's grief book addressing the questions a child may pose after the loss of a loved one.

Susie Q's Kids Positive Reflections: Good Characteristics Coloring Book

- A children's coloring book reflecting on the positive aspects a child should model.

POSITIVE REFLECTION TEAM – CARRY ON THE CONVERSATION

https://drmarywelsh.com/

Imagine Dr. Mary Welsh, Author and Grief Session Facilitator, or one of her Certified Coaches leading you on your transformational journey through your loss and aiding you in finding a sense of healing with a passion and purpose in your 'new normal.'

Envision understanding you are not alone; you have a past and a future. We encourage you on your journey as you Remember ◊ Reflect ◊ Recreate ◊ Relate. Your passport to self-help and discovery continues with participation in this program.

Imagine being able to find comfort in dialogue with others traveling their journeys to find peace with their loss, and a new passion and purpose. Participants can join from anywhere in the world. What is the cost of not finding a sense of peace and your new potential?

The Positive Reflection Team is a community of members seeking to understand the depth of loss from grief or adversity and how they can embrace their new normal. This monthly membership site provides audio teachings, video courses, articles and insights along with a private Facebook page to connect with other like-minded individuals. who offer support, encouragement, compassion and a presence of accountability on your journey, and interactions with author and coach Dr. Mary Welsh.

Coaching Services – Extend the Conversation

https://drmarywelsh.com/

Enrollment in a private Facebook group environment to share your stories, your challenges, and to look for guidance from others that have embarked on the same type of journey. Finding a community of peers that understand your frustrations, anger, anxiety, and heartbreak, gives you the potential to inspire, support, and strengthen your resolve to lead a better life while still honoring your loved ones. Join our group today!

Apply for my personalized coaching. Connecting with Dr. Mary Welsh as your coach and grief session facilitator will help guide you through the painful journey of self-help and discovery. Through her 1:1 coaching services, you receive focused teachings and live 1:1 coaching to further your healing journey.

NEED A SPEAKER, CONTACT DR. MARY

https://drmarywelsh.com/

Do you need a speaker? Does your group need to understand the potential of overcoming loss, whether in their personal or professional lives? Overcoming the challenges of life can be overwhelming.

Author and National Speaker, Dr. Mary Welsh speaks from the heart, sharing her stories, and how to look for the positive in any situation. These reflections enable a person to embody a different positive perspective than the negative self-talk of being a victim or injured party.

Life is full of lessons, overcoming the loss of a child positions someone to pick up the pieces of a world torn apart and find the ability to live again with a 'new normal.' Learn to overcome any type of adversity from her outlook on keeping a positive viewpoint.

Speaking engagements include:
- Compassionate Friends 2020 National Conference
- Bereaved Parents of USA 2020 National Conference

Contact Dr. Mary Welsh today, her message of positivity, passion, and finding purpose is powerful!

Q's Give Back Program - Susie Q's Kids "One Comfort Bag at a Time"

https://drmarywelsh.com/
https://susieqskids.org/

Susie Q's Kids was started to honor Susan McBride-Welsh (Susie Q) a special young lady who loved kids, giving back, and living every day to its fullest. All kids need comfort. Imagine the smile as the kids we help find inspiration and comfort in the contents of our special comfort bags.

Susie Q's Kids is committed to brightening and inspiring the lives of children and young adults, "One Bag at a Time." Make a difference, support our cause, every contribution helps to brighten and inspire the lives of a child or young adult. Our bags are distributed to other nonprofits for distribution to hospitals, foster care, shelters, and grieving groups. Learn more by visiting our website https://susieqskids.org/. Donate now!

Q's Thumbs Up Revolution – Be Inspired

https://drmarywelsh.com/
https://www.facebook.com/Thumbs-Up-Revolution

Imagine a life full of positivity and an appreciation for the past, the present, and the future. A simple geture such as 'a thumbs up' can signify 'you can do it' or 'good job', and provide positive reinforcement.

Our family and friends extend a thumbs up in our photo opportunities to recognize our loved one Susie is with us always. When we look back on the pictures, we can see her in all our life's events captured in our pictures with a simple thumbs up gesture.

Join the Thumbs Up Revolution. Post your pictures and a brief caption of the event or person recognized with your thumbs up.

Q's Inspirational Essentials – Get Inspired

https://drmarywelsh.com/

Envision a weekly inspirational quote to encompass the varying feelings you may have upon your life's journey. Look to others for inspiration from these quotes and how they inspire them to be their best. Recognize the value of positive verses, meditations, and considerations. Add your thoughts, reflections, and considerations to further your healing path of self-help and discovery.

Dream big, expand your beliefs to embrace the value of positivity along your journey to heal your soul, your heart, and your outlook. Get inspired today! Register at https://drmarywelsh.com/ to get your weekly update.

APPENDIX D
CONTACT LIST (*WEBSITES AND NUMBERS MAY CHANGE)

AMERICAN FOUNDATION FOR SUICIDE AWARENESS (AFSP)

https://afsp.org/

AFSP raises awareness, funds scientific research and provides resources and aid to those affected by suicide.

They do not provide their own crisis hotline service. If you are in crisis, please call the National Suicide Prevention Lifeline at 1-800-273-8255 or contact the Crisis Text Line by texting TALK to 741741.

THE NATIONAL SUICIDE PREVENTION LIFELINE AT 1-800-273-TALK (8255).

National Institute of Mental Health website: https://www.nimh.nih.gov/health/publications/suicide-faq/index.shtml.

Call the toll-free National Suicide Prevention Lifeline (NSPL) at 1–800–273–TALK (8255), 24 hours a day, 7 days a week. The service is available to everyone.

The deaf and hard of hearing can contact the Lifeline via TTY at 1–800–799–4889.

Nation Suicide Prevention Lifeline (NSPL) website. The Crisis Text Line is another resource available 24 hours a day, 7 days a week. Text "home" to 741741.

BEREAVED PARENTS OF THE USA

https://www.bereavedparentsusa.org

Bereaved Parents of the USA is a non-profit self-help group that offers support to bereaved families struggling to rebuild their lives after the death of family. Visit their website to learn about your local chapter.

COMPASSIONATE FRIENDS

https://www.compassionatefriends.org

The Compassionate Friends non-profit organization exists to provide friendship, understanding, and hope to those going through the natural grieving process. Visit their website to learn about your local chapter.

TRAGEDY ASSISTANCE PROGRAM FOR SURVIVORS (TAPS)

https://www.taps.org/

The Tragedy Assistance Program for Survivors (TAPS) offers compassionate care to all those grieving the loss of a loved one who died while serving in our Armed Forces or as a result of his or her service. Since 1994, TAPS has provided comfort and hope 24/7 through a national peer support network and connection to grief resources, all at no cost to surviving families and loved ones.

If you are grieving the loss of a fallen service member, or if you know someone who can use our support, the **TAPS 24/7 National Military Survivor Helpline** is always available toll-free with loving support and resources at 800-959-TAPS (8277).

Visit their website to learn about their programs and national and local chapters.

SUSIE Q'S KIDS

https://susieqskids.org/

Susie Q's Kids was started in honor of Susie (Q) McBride-Welsh. The purpose is to brighten and inspire the lives of children and young adults "One Comfort Bag at a Time" and to raise awareness for other nonprofits that partner with us to distribute the comfort bags to children in hospitals, shelters, foster care, grieving groups, where ever there is a need.

Email: drmary@susieqskids.org

Phone: 248-220-6846

DR. MARY WELSH

Dr. Mary offers Grief Facilitation Coaching.

Visit her website to learn more about her services: https://drmarywelsh.com

Email: drmary@drmarywelsh.com

Phone: 586-206-8424

APPENDIX E
BIBLIOGRAPHY

1   Eisenhower, D. (n.d.). Retrieved from https://quotefancy.
     com/quote/796636/Dwight-D-Eisenhower-There-s-n
     o-tragedy-in-life-like-the-death-of-a-child-Things-never-get.

2   Recover from Grief (2018). 7 Stages of grief through
     the process and back to life. Retrieved from www.
     recover-from-grief.com/7-stages-of-grief.html.

3   Tolstoy, L. (n.d.). Goodreads quotes. Retrieved from https://
     www.goodreads.com/quotes/36797-only-people-who-are-c
     apable-of-loving-strongly-can-also.

4   Recover from Grief. (2018). 7 Stages of grief through the
     process and back to life. Shock and denial. Retrieved from
     www.recover-from-grief.com/7-stages-of-grief.html.

5   Recover from Grief. (2018). 7 Stages of grief through the
     process and back to life. Pain and guilt. Retrieved from www.
     recover-from-grief.com/7-stages-of-grief.html.

6   Recover from Grief. (2018). 7 Stages of grief through the
     process and back to life. Anger and bargaining. Retrieved from
     www.recover-from-grief.com/7-stages-of-grief.html.

7   Recover from Grief. (2018). 7 Stages of grief through
     the process and back to life. Depression, reflection and

loneliness. Retrieved from www.recover-from-grief.com/7-stages-of-grief.html.

[8] Recover from Grief. (2018). 7 Stages of grief through the process and back to life. The upward turn. Retrieved from www.recover-from-grief.com/7-stages-of-grief.html.

[9] Recover from Grief. (2018). 7 Stages of grief through the process and back to life. Reconstruction and working through. Retrieved from www.recover-from-grief.com/7-stages-of-grief.html.

[10] Stephen Ministries. (2014). A Time to grieve. Journeying through grief—Book 1 excerpt. The fog of grief. Retrieved from https://www.stephenministries.org/griefresources/default.cfm/765.

[11] Recover from Grief. (2018). 7 Stages of grief through the process and back to life. Acceptance and hope. Retrieved from www.recover-from-grief.com/7-stages-of-grief.html.

[12] Long, E. (Jun. 23, 2015). Good Therapy Blog: 4 things you need to know about moving on from grief. Retrieved from https://www.goodtherapy.org/blog/4-things-you-need-to-know-about-moving-on-from-grief-0623155.

[13] Miyazawa, K. (n.d.) Good Reads quotes. Retrieved from https://www.goodreads.com/quotes/35468-we-must-embrace-pain-and-burn-it-as-fuel-for.

[14] Alexander, V. (n.d.). Grief Speaks quotes. Retrieved from http://www.griefspeaks.com/id112.html.

[15] Ford, T. (n.d.) Hope Grows: Making connections with others is among the most important things in life. Retrieved from https://hopegrows.net/news/making-connections-most-important-things-in-life.

[16] Alexander, V. (1991). In the wake of suicide: stories of the people left behind. Jossey-Bass. Retrieved from https://libquotes.com/victoria-alexander/quote/lbd3y8c.

17   Good therapy. (Dec. 12, 2016). Life Purpose. Retrieved from https://www.goodtherapy.org/learn-about-therapy/issues/life-purpose.

18   Beth, K. (Oct.4, 2013). Finding the grace within: Healing, the power of release. Retrieved from http://www.findingthegracewithin.com/the-weight-of-release/.

19   Wolfelt, A. (n.d.). Batesville: Nurturing yourself when grieving. Retrieved from https://www.batesville.com/be-kind-to-yourself/.

20   Wolfelt, A. (Dec. 14, 2016). Center for loss and life transition: Nurturing yourself when you're grieving. Retrieved from https://www.centerforloss.com/2016/12/nurturing-youre-grieving/.

21   Wolfelt, A. (Dec. 14, 2016). Center for loss and life transition: Nurturing yourself when you're grieving. Retrieved from https://www.centerforloss.com/2016/12/nurturing-youre-grieving/.

22   Healthline. (Jun. 29, 2018). Retrieved from https://www.healthline.com/nutrition/10-reasons-why-good-sleep-is-important.

23   What's your grief blog. (Apr. 10, 2018). Retrieved from: https://whatsyourgrief.com/death-of-a-sibling/.

24   Wilde, O.(n.d.). Good reads quotes. Retrieved from https://www.goodreads.com/quotes/2448-to-live-is-the-rarest-thing-in-the-world-most.

25   What's your grief blog. (2019). Grief makes you feel like you're going crazy. Retrieved from https://www.centerforloss.com/2016/12/nurturing-youre-grieving/.

26   What's your grief blog. (2019). Grief makes you feel like you're going crazy. Retrieved from https://www.centerforloss.com/2016/12/nurturing-youre-grieving/.

27   What's your grief blog. (2019). Grief makes you feel like you're going crazy. Retrieved from https://www.centerforloss.com/2016/12/nurturing-youre-grieving/.

28 Myers, B. & Zanda-Hilger, M. Family Caregiver Education, Area Agency on Aging, Revised by Zanda Hilger and Betty Purkey, (revised April, 2017.) Grief and loss: Grief explored. Retrieved from https://www.familycaregiversonline.net/wp-content/uploads/GriefLossREV2017.pdf.

29 Wortman & Latack (2015). What's your grief blog: Grieving a suicide death. Retrieved from https://whatsyourgrief.com/grieving-suicide-death/.

30 Moorhead, J. (Mar., 2017) The Guardian: Family How to live and learn from great loss. Retrieved from https://whatsyourgrief.com/grieving-suicide-death/.

31 Senior Citizen's Guide to Pittsburgh. (n.d.). Grief support for older adults- A much needed resource. Retrieved from https://www.seniorcitizensguide.com/articles/pittsburgh/grief-support-older-adults.html.

32 Bekker, T. (Oct. 16, 2013). Green Bay Oncology blog: Gender difference in grief. Retrieved from https://gboncology.com/blog/gender-differences-in-grief/.

33 Bekker, T. (Oct. 16, 2013). Green Bay Oncology blog: Gender difference in grief. Retrieved from https://gboncology.com/blog/gender-differences-in-grief/.

34 Morrisey, B. (Jul. 28, 2018). Facing bereavement: Coping with miscarriage. Retrieved from http://www.facingbereavement.co.uk/CopingMiscarriage.html.

35 Morrisey, B. (Jul. 28, 2018). Facing bereavement: Coping with miscarriage. Retrieved from http://www.facingbereavement.co.uk/CopingMiscarriage.html.

36 Skylight. (2017). Kids health: Bereavement reactions by age group. Retrieved from https://www.kidshealth.org.nz/bereavement-reactions-age-group.

37 Skylight. (2017). Kids health: Bereavement reactions by age group. Retrieved from https://www.kidshealth.org.nz/bereavement-reactions-age-group.

38 Skylight. (2017). Kids health: Bereavement reactions by age group. Retrieved from https://www.kidshealth.org.nz/bereavement-reactions-age-group.

39 Skylight. (2017). Kids health: Bereavement reactions by age group. Retrieved from https://www.kidshealth.org.nz/bereavement-reactions-age-group.

40 Phillips Lifeline. (May 20, 2014). Grief vs. depression in the elderly: what's really going on? Retrieved from https://www.lifeline.philips.com/resources/blog/2014/05/grief-vs-depression-in-the-elderly-whats-really-going-on.html.

41 Senior Citizen's Guide to Pittsburgh. (n.d.). Grief support for older adults- A much needed resource. Retrieved from https://www.seniorcitizensguide.com/articles/pittsburgh/grief-support-older-adults.html.

42 What's your grief? (Apr. 10, 2019) Grieving the death of a sibling. Retrieved from https://whatsyourgrief.com/death-of-a-sibling/.

43 Author unknown. (Jun. 3, 2017). U.S. Department of Health & Human Services National Institute on Aging: Mourning the death of a spouse. Retrieved from https://www.nia.nih.gov/health/mourning-death-spouse.

44 Senior Citizen's Guide to Pittsburgh. (n.d.). Grief support for older adults- A much needed resource. Retrieved from https://www.seniorcitizensguide.com/articles/pittsburgh/grief-support-older-adults.html.

45 Shock, N. (n.d.). Encyclopedia Britannica. Human gaining: Physiology and sociology. Retrieved from https://www.britannica.com/science/human-aging.

46 Staudacher, C. (n.d.). Belief Net inspire your everyday. Surviving a violent death: When accident, suicide or murder claim a loved one, how do you cope? Retrieved from https://www.beliefnet.com/love-family/2000/05/surviving-a-violent-death.aspx?

47 Staudacher, C. (n.d.). Belief Net inspire your everyday. Surviving a violent death: When accident, suicide or murder claim a loved one, how do you cope? Retrieved from https://www.beliefnet.com/love-family/2000/05/surviving-a-violent-death.aspx?

48 Staudacher, C. (n.d.). Belief Net inspire your everyday. Surviving a violent death: When accident, suicide or murder claim a loved one, how do you cope? Retrieved from https://www.beliefnet.com/love-family/2000/05/surviving-a-violent-death.aspx?

49 Myers, B. & Zanda-Hilger, M. Family Caregiver Education, Area Agency on Aging, Revised by Zanda Hilger and Betty Purkey, (revised April, 2017.) Grief and loss: Grief explored. Retrieved from https://www.familycaregiversonline.net/wp-content/uploads/GriefLossREV2017.pdf.

50 What's your grief blog. (n.d.). Grieving a suicide death. (Jamison, K. n.d. Night Falls Fast: Understanding Suicide) Retrieved from https://whatsyourgrief.com/grieving-suicide-death/.

51 What's your grief blog. (n.d.). Grieving a suicide death. Retrieved from https://whatsyourgrief.com/grieving-suicide-death/.

52 Morrisey, B. (Jul. 28, 2018). Facing bereavement: Coping with miscarriage. Retrieved from http://www.facingbereavement.co.uk/coping-with-death-through-accidents.html.

53 Grief speaks. (n.d.). Murder or homicide. Retrieved from http://www.griefspeaks.com/id82.html.

54 Grief speaks. (n.d.). Murder or homicide. Retrieved from http://www.griefspeaks.com/id82.html.

55 Grief speaks. (n.d.). or homicide. Retrieved from http://www.griefspeaks.com/id82.html.

56 Fowler, J. (Aug. 31, 2017).ASD: 7 ways grief is compounded by an overdose death. Retrieved from https://www.myasd. com/blog/7-ways-grief-compounded-overdose-death.

57 Harvard health publishing. (n.d.). Harvard medical school. Healthbeat: Easing grief through religion and spirituality. Retrieved from https://www.health.harvard.edu/ mind-and-mood/easing-grief-through-religion-and-spirituality.

58 Cremation resource. (n.d.). How to decide whether to cremate or bury? Retrieved from https://www.health.harvard.edu/ mind-and-mood/easing-grief-through-religion-and-spirituality.

59 Keen. (n.d.). Renewing your life after a loved one's death. Retrieved from https://www.keen.com/articles/spiritual/ renewing-your-life-after-a-loved-ones-death.

60 Richardson, J. (n.d.). Love lives on: Surviving the grief of an overdose death. Retrieved from https://www.loveliveson.com/ surviving-the-grief-of-an-overdose-death/.

61 National institute of mental health, (n.d.). Suicide in America: Frequently asked questions. Retrieved from https:// www.nimh.nih.gov/health/publications/suicide-faq/index. shtml.

62 Bergen, A. (Jul. 6, 2018). Lateral leadership: When life forces you hand, embrace the new chapter. Retrieved from https:// lateralleadership.wordpress.com/tag/change/.

63 Plato (n.d.). AZ quotes. Retrieved from https://www.azquotes. com/quote/922197.

64 Author unknown. (n.d.). From Dad's perspective.

65 Author unknown. (n.d.). From Dad's perspective.

Made in the USA
Monee, IL
31 May 2020